Best Easy Day Hikes
Springfield, Missouri

Help Us Keep This Guide Up to Date

Every effort has been made by the author and editors to make this guide as accurate and useful as possible. However, many things can change after a guide is published—trails are rerouted, regulations change, facilities come under new management, etc.

We would love to hear from you concerning your experiences with this guide and how you feel it could be improved and kept up to date. While we may not be able to respond to all comments and suggestions, we'll take them to heart and we'll also make certain to share them with the authors. Please send your comments and suggestions to the following address:

Globe Pequot Press
Reader Response/Editorial Department
PO Box 480
Guilford, CT 06437

Or you may e-mail us at:

editorial@GlobePequot.com

Thanks for your input, and happy trails!

Best Easy Day Hikes Series

Best Easy Day Hikes Springfield, Missouri

JD Tanner and Emily Ressler-Tanner

FALCONGUIDES

GUILFORD, CONNECTICUT
HELENA, MONTANA
AN IMPRINT OF GLOBE PEQUOT PRESS

To buy books in quantity for corporate use
or incentives, call **(800) 962-0973**
or e-mail **premiums@GlobePequot.com**.

FALCONGUIDES®

Project editor: David Legere
Layout: Kirsten Livingston
Maps by Design Maps Inc. © Morris Book Publishing, LLC

TOPO! Explorer software and SuperQuad source maps courtesy of
National Geographic Maps. For information about TOPO! Explorer,
TOPO!, and Nat Geo Maps products, go to www.topo.com or www
.natgeomaps.com.

Library of Congress Cataloging-in-Publication Data is available on file.

ISBN 978-0-7627-6353-5

Printed in the United States of America

10 9 8 7 6 5 4 3 2 1

Contents

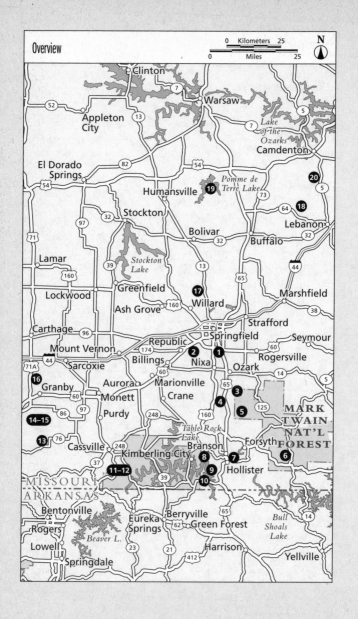

Acknowledgments

We would like to send out a special thank-you to all the land managers who patiently answered our questions, pointed us toward the very best trails, and carefully reviewed the trail descriptions for this guide. We would also like to thank our friends and family for accompanying us on many of the trails in and around Springfield; your company, humor, support, and enthusiasm were very much appreciated. Finally we would like to thank all our friends at FalconGuides, particularly Katie Benoit, Max Phelps, and Jessica Haberman, for their support, encouragement, and making a book out of our rough manuscript.

Introduction

Springfield sits in the southwest portion of the state and lies in the heart of the Missouri Ozarks. If you are not from Springfield or have never been to the city, it is one of those places that will make you say, "I had no idea all of this was here." The rolling hills of the Ozarks, the rich history of the area, a surprisingly green city, and access to numerous outdoor adventure activities will have you coming back for more.

This guide lists easy, moderate, and more challenging hikes within 100 miles of Springfield, Missouri. Some of the hikes can be found within the city of Springfield; others are located just outside the city in the surrounding Ozarks of southwestern Missouri.

The city of Springfield was incorporated in 1838 and has taken on numerous nicknames including the Queen City of the Ozarks, the Gateway to the Ozarks, and the Birthplace of Route 66. Today the Springfield area population is over 200,000, making it the third-largest city in Missouri. The city is the home of Bass Pro Shops, boasts attractions like Wilson's Creek National Battlefield and Fantastic Caverns, and provides access to the sights and sounds of Branson.

The Ozarks extend south, east, and west from Springfield throughout southern Missouri into northern Arkansas, eastern Oklahoma, and southeastern Kansas. The ecologically diverse, hilly, and sometimes rugged Ozarks not only offer great hiking but also provide many opportunities for canoeing, rock climbing, horseback riding, and much, much more.

Featured in the pages of this book are twenty of the best easy day hikes in and around Springfield. We have done our best to include a little of something for everyone. Hikes for families, for birding, for scenic views, for trail runners, and for pets have all been included. Consider these hikes an introduction to the areas and a starting point to continue your explorations.

The Nature of Springfield

Springfield area trails range from rugged and hilly to flat and paved. Hikes in this guide cover a little bit of everything. While by definition a best easy day hike is not strenuous and poses little danger to the traveler, knowing a few details about the nature of the Springfield area will only enhance your explorations.

Weather

Have you ever heard the expression, "If you don't like the weather, just wait five minutes?" Well, people in southwestern Missouri say it too.

Spring in the Springfield area is mild, ranging from cool to warm and muggy, and is typically wet. Trail conditions can be quite muddy during spring, especially for hikes that are in or near floodplains. During spring the greatest weather concern is the chance for thunder/lightning storms, hail, and/or tornadoes.

Storms still pose a threat in early summer, but as summer progresses the weather tends to be less wet and is sometimes very hot and almost always humid. Hikers who choose to get out in mid to late summer might consider early-morning hikes, as high temperatures and humidity usually set in by midmorning.

Fall can be downright gorgeous in Springfield and the surrounding Ozarks. Daytime temperatures in the low to mid 70s along with the fall foliage can result in some amazing scenic hikes. Fall hiking cannot be encouraged enough.

Springfield has its fair share of cold and snowy days in winter, but if you don't mind having no leaves on the trees, winter can be a very enjoyable time to hike here as well. Hikers in winter will get more views of the rolling Ozarks and will typically enjoy the trails almost all to themselves.

Ideal times for hiking in Springfield are early to late spring and mid to late fall. Mix in the handful of cool days in summer and warm winter days, and there are many ideal hiking days per year in Springfield.

Hazards

There are a few hazards to be aware of and to prepare for when hiking in the Springfield area. Poison ivy, a year-round hazard, might be the most common and most annoying issue hikers will come across. Poison ivy has been found in every county in Missouri, and it is estimated that somewhere between 50 to 70 percent of people experience a physical reaction after coming in contact with the plant. Poison ivy can grow as a woody shrub up to 6 feet high or as a vine that clings to other trees and shrubs. While the old expression "Leaves of three, let it be" is good advice to follow, several other three-leaf plants grow in the Springfield area, so be sure to educate yourself about poison ivy before hitting the trail. Poison ivy can be found on almost every hike in this book.

Ticks are most abundant in Springfield during spring and summer. There are many different types of ticks, but the two most common in Missouri are the Lone Star tick and the American dog tick. Ticks have been known to carry—and occasionally spread—the organisms that cause Lyme disease, Rocky Mountain spotted fever, and tularemia. Ticks are unavoidable but are no reason to avoid hiking in spring and summer. Hikers should wear lighter colored clothing to help detect ticks, use repellent that is proven effective against ticks, periodically check for ticks during your hike, and perform a complete body check of yourself and your pet after every hike. During spring and summer, ticks can be found on every hike in this book.

There are fifty different species of mosquitoes in Missouri, and the most common concern with mosquitoes is the West Nile virus. It is estimated that only 1 percent of mosquitoes carry the West Nile virus and only 1 percent of people bitten will actually contract the virus. Like ticks, mosquitoes should not be a reason to avoid hiking in spring or summer. Simply be aware and be prepared. To help you avoid mosquitoes, use insect repellent, wear long pants and long-sleeved shirts, avoid hiking at dawn or dusk, and don't wear perfume or cologne when hiking. Mosquitoes can be found on every hike in this book.

Venomous snakes are the fourth hazard hikers might encounter on the hikes in this book. Most of the snakes in the Springfield area are harmless; however, hikers should be aware that several species of venomous snakes do inhabit the area. Your chances of being bitten by a venomous snake in the United States are very, very low. Fewer than 8,000 people are bitten every year by a venomous snake, most while trying to handle or kill the snake, and fewer than five of those people die. Missouri is home to five species of venomous snakes. The Osage copperhead, western cottonmouth (water moccasin), timber rattlesnake, eastern Massasauga rattlesnake (swamp rattler), and western pygmy rattlesnake (ground rattler) can all be found in or near the Springfield area. The Osage copperhead and timber rattlesnake are the venomous snakes a hiker is most likely to encounter. Venomous snakes are most commonly recognized by their "arrow-shaped" heads. Three of the five venomous snakes in Missouri are rattlesnakes and can be easily identified by the rattling noise they make when threatened. To avoid being bitten, hikers should wear protective footwear, never place hands under rocks or logs, keep an eye on the ground as they hike, and never attempt to handle or kill snakes.

Other hazards you may encounter include (but are not limited to) drop-offs along bluffs, thunder/lightning storms, tornadoes, a growing population of black bears, and heat-related illnesses.

Be Prepared

"Be prepared." The Boy Scouts say it, the Leave No Trace organization says it, and the best outdoors people say it. Being prepared won't completely keep you out of harm's way when outdoors, but it will minimize the chances of finding yourself there. Here are some things to consider:

- Familiarize yourself with the basics of first aid (bites, stings, sprains, and breaks), carry a first-aid kit, and know how to use it.
- Hydrate! No matter where or when you are hiking, you should always carry water with you. A standard is two liters per person per day.

- Be prepared to treat water on longer hikes. It is not safe to drink untreated water from rivers and streams in the Springfield area. Iodine tablets are small, light, and easy to carry.

- Carry a backpack in order to store the Ten Essentials: map, compass, sunglasses/sunscreen, extra food and water, extra clothes, headlamp/flashlight, first-aid kit, fire starter, matches, and knife.

- Pack your cell phone (on vibrate) as a safety backup.

- Keep an eye on the kids. Have them carry a whistle to help you locate them, just in case they wander off.

- Bring a leash, plastic bags for dog waste, and extra water for your pets.

Leave No Trace

This hiking guide will take you to historical sites, conservation areas, national natural landmarks, and many other places of natural and cultural significance. For that reason, the importance of following the principles of Leave No Trace cannot be stressed enough.

Do your best to stick to trails to avoid inadvertently trampling sensitive vegetation. Be prepared to pack out any trash you bring with you, and remember that it never hurts to carry out trash that others have left behind. Be extra careful when visiting sites of historical and natural importance. Leave everything as you found it, and never remove artifacts from these sensitive areas.

Consider your impact on wildlife living in the environment in which you hike, and be sure not to feed wild animals, an act that is unhealthy for wildlife and dangerous for people. Respect other visitors and trail users by keeping your pets on a leash, stepping to the side of the trail to allow others to pass, and keeping noise to a minimum.

For more information on enjoying the outdoors responsibly, please visit the Leave No Trace Center for Outdoor Ethics website at www.LNT.org.

Land Management

The following agencies manage the public lands where the hikes in this book are located. Contact them with any questions and concerns before visiting or while planning your visit:

Branson Parks and Recreation, 1500 Branson Hills Parkway, Branson, MO 65616; (417) 335-2368; www.bransonparksandrecreation.com

Missouri Department of Natural Resources, PO Box 176, Jefferson City, MO 65102; (573) 751-3443 or (800) 361-4827; www.dnr.mo.gov

Missouri Department of Conservation, Conservation Headquarters, 2901 West Truman Blvd., Jefferson City, MO; (573) 522-4115; http://mdc.mo.gov

Missouri Department of Natural Resources, Division of State Parks, PO Box 176, Jefferson City, MO 65102; (800) 361-4827 or (573) 751-3443; http://mostateparks.com

National Park Service, www.nps.gov

Keep in mind that from the time this book was published to the time that you are reading it, some land management rules and regulations may have already changed. Always check for new and updated information about the area you plan to visit.

How to Use This Guide

This guide is designed to be simple and easy to use. Each hike is described with a map and summary information that delivers the trail's vital statistics including length, difficulty, fees and permits, park hours, canine compatibility, and trail contacts. Directions to the trailhead are also provided, along with a general description of what you'll see along the way. A detailed route finder (Miles and Directions) sets forth mileages between significant landmarks along the trail.

How the Hikes Were Chosen

This guide describes trails that are accessible to every hiker, whether out-of-town visitor or local resident. The hikes are no longer than 6 miles round-trip, and most are considerably shorter. They range in difficulty from flat excursions perfect for a family outing to more challenging treks in the rolling hills of the Ozarks. While these trails are among the best, keep in mind that nearby trails, sometimes in the same park or in a neighboring open space, may offer options better suited to your needs. We've selected hikes in the immediate Springfield metropolitan area, the Branson area, and the western Missouri Ozarks—wherever your starting point, you'll find a great easy day hike nearby.

Selecting a Hike

These are all easy hikes, but easy is a relative term. Some would argue that no hike involving any kind of climbing is easy, but climbs are a fact of life in the Springfield area.

Easy hikes are generally short and flat, taking no longer than an hour to complete.

Moderate hikes involve increased distance and relatively mild changes in elevation and will take one to two hours to complete.

More challenging hikes feature some steep stretches and greater distances and generally take longer than two hours to complete.

Keep in mind that what you think is easy is entirely dependent on your level of fitness and the adequacy of your gear (primarily shoes). Use the trail's length as a gauge of its relative difficulty—even if climbing is involved, it won't be too strenuous if the hike is less than 1 mile long. The Trail Finder lists Best Long Hikes, which are more challenging than others due to length and elevation changes. If you are hiking with a group, select a hike that's appropriate for the least fit and prepared in your party.

Hiking times are based on the assumption that on flat ground, most walkers average 2 miles per hour. Adjust that rate by the steepness of the terrain and your level of fitness (subtract time if you're an aerobic animal and add time if you're hiking with kids), and you have a ballpark hiking duration. Be sure to add more time if you plan to picnic or take part in other activities like birding or photography.

Trail Finder

Best Hikes for Birders

Best Hikes with Children

Best Hikes with Dogs

Best Hikes for Great Views

Best Hikes for Nature Lovers

Best Hikes for History Buffs

Map Legend

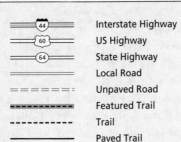

44	Interstate Highway
60	US Highway
64	State Highway
	Local Road
	Unpaved Road
	Featured Trail
	Trail
	Paved Trail
	River/Creek
	State Park/County Park/Preserve
	National Forest/National Park
‿	Bridge
IIIIIIIIIIII	Boardwalk/Steps
▲	Camping
🅿	Parking
	Picnic Area
■	Point of Interest/Structure
	Restroom
○	Town
11	Trailhead
	Viewpoint/Overlook
⌀	Spring
?	Visitor/Information Center
	Tower
	Stables

1 Springfield Conservation Nature Center Trails

Located within the Springfield city limits, the Springfield Conservation Nature Center is a spectacular resource for people hoping to learn more about the nature of southwestern Missouri. In addition to the stellar educational and interpretive information and programs offered here, the Springfield Conservation Nature Center also offers several options for hiking. Linked together, these trails make a fantastic loop hike.

Distance: 2.25-mile loop
Hiking time: About 1.5 hours
Difficulty: Moderate due to length
Best season: Year-round
Other trail users: Trail runners
Canine compatibility: Dogs prohibited
Fees and permits: No fees or permits required
Schedule: Grounds open 8 a.m. to 8 p.m. Mar 1 through Oct 31 and 8 a.m. to 6 p.m. Nov 1 through Feb 28. Building open 8 a.m. to 5 p.m. Tues through Sat and noon to 5 p.m. Sun, closed Mon (Mar 1 through Oct 31); open Tues through Sat 8 a.m. to 5 p.m., closed Sun and Mon (Nov 1 through Feb 29). Nature center buildings and trails closed on New Year's Day, Thanksgiving, and Christmas.
Maps: USGS Galloway; detailed trail map and brochure available at the visitor center
Trail contacts: Springfield Conservation Nature Center, 4601 South Nature Center Way, Springfield, MO 65804-4920; (417) 888-4237; http://mdc .mo.gov/regions/southwest/ springfield-conservation-nature-center
Special considerations: Jogging/running is limited to posted hours.

Finding the trailhead: From the intersection of I-44 and US 65, take US 65 south to the US 65 Business/US 60 W/James River Freeway exit. Merge onto US 60 W/US 65 Business N and travel 1.1 miles. Take the US 65 Business /Glenstone Avenue exit toward Republic Road and turn left (south) onto South Glenstone Avenue. Take the first left onto South Nature Center Way and travel about 1 mile to the park entrance. Drive through the park gates into the visitor center parking area. The trailhead and restrooms are located at the southeast corner of the parking area. GPS: N37 7.703' / W93 14.376'

The Hike

Managed by the Missouri Department of Conservation, the Springfield Conservation Nature Center is a great place to spend the day. Inside the nature center, visitors will find programs, activities, and displays that focus on the nature of the Ozarks. Offering a wide range of activities that are geared to children, teens, adults, and families, the nature center is an incredible resource for nature enthusiasts living in or visiting the area.

Outside the nature center, visitors will enjoy exploring the 80-acre conservation area. As you wander along the trails you may forget that you are within the Springfield city limits. The flora, fauna, and landscape here are much like what you would expect to see anywhere in the Ozarks. Hikers will likely encounter lots of wildlife along the trails: white-tailed deer, wild turkey, eastern gray squirrel, bullfrogs, and box turtles are common sights here. Fox, mink, muskrat, beaver, raccoon, and other Ozark critters also can be found here, although they may be a bit more challenging to spot. Visit anytime except winter and you are sure to see a dazzling array of wildflowers, including purple coneflower and Queen Anne's lace.

While there are several short, easy trails in the conservation area, the 2.25-mile outer loop allows visitors to gain a broader appreciation of the natural diversity of the area. To begin this hike, locate the Savanna Ridge trailhead, which is northeast of the nature center, just beyond the restroom.

Begin hiking northeast on the paved Savanna Ridge Trail. At 0.1 mile come to a fork in the trail; stay left (northwest) and the trail soon skirts the southern end of a small savanna—a prairie landscape of mostly grasses and wildflowers and a scattering of trees. At 0.2 mile the trail forks again. Turn left (northeast) onto the gravel path known as the Long Trail. The Long Trail will take you through most of the conservation area, crossing through upland and bottomland forests, marshes, prairielike grasslands, and glades. At 0.5 mile come to a boardwalk that allows you to cross a marshy area without getting your feet wet. Cross a footbridge over Galloway Creek (0.7 mile) and then come to the intersection of the Galloway Creek Greenway Trail at 0.9 mile. The Galloway Creek Greenway Trail is part of the Ozark Greenways trail network, which is a series of nonmotorized, multiuser trails that run throughout Springfield. These hard-surfaced trails are popular with runners, bikers, and walkers.

At 1.1 miles come to the intersection with the Photo Blind Trail; continue northwest to stay on the Long Trail and cross Long Bridge, which spans Lake Springfield. Once across the bridge (1.2 miles), bear left (west), continuing on the Long Trail until it joins the Fox Bluff Trail at 1.9 miles. Here the trail splits; stay left (southeast). Very shortly come

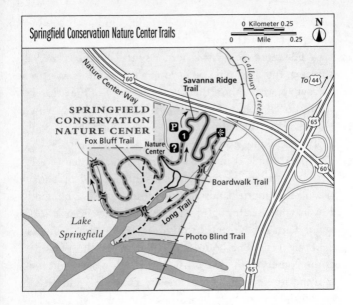

to another fork in the trail; stay left (north) until the Fox Bluff Trail joins the Boardwalk Trail at 2.1 miles.

Follow the Boardwalk Trail east then north as it passes the nature center and returns to the Savanna Ridge trailhead at 2.25 miles.

Miles and Directions

- **0.0** Start northeast of the Springfield Conservation Nature Center and head northeast on the paved Savanna Ridge Trail.
- **0.1** Come to a fork in the trail; stay left (northwest).
- **0.2** Come to a second fork; turn left (northeast) onto the gravel path known as the Long Trail.
- **0.7** Cross Galloway Creek; continue southwest.
- **0.9** Come to the intersection of the Galloway Creek Greenway Trail; continue southwest.

1.1 Intersect the Photo Blind Trail; continue northwest to stay on the Long Trail and cross Long Bridge.

1.2 After crossing Long Bridge, turn left (west).

1.9 Long Trail joins Fox Bluff Trail; stay left (southeast) at the fork. Very shortly come to another fork in the trail; stay left (north).

2.1 Fox Bluff Trail joins the Boardwalk Trail; continue east.

2.25 Arrive back at the Savanna Ridge trailhead.

2 Wilson's Creek National Battlefield: Bloody Hill to Wire Road Trail

This easy stroll offers a glimpse into Missouri's role as a border state during the Civil War. In addition to learning about the historical significance of the area, hikers will experience a wide variety of wildflowers, trees, and wildlife common in this part of the Ozarks.

Distance: 2.2-mile loop

Hiking time: About 1 hour

Difficulty: Easy; mostly flat terrain

Best season: Fall through spring

Other trail users: Equestrians; bicyclists and cars allowed on the auto road

Canine compatibility: Leashed dogs permitted

Fees and permits: Small fee required

Schedule: Visitor center open daily from 8 a.m. to 5 p.m. Museum open daily from 9 a.m. to 4 p.m. Apr through Nov (closed Dec through Mar). Park (Tour Road) open daily from 8 a.m. to 9 p.m. All areas closed at noon on Christmas Eve and all day Thanksgiving, Christmas, and New Year's Day.

Maps: USGS Republic; interpretive trail map available at the visitor center

Trail contacts: Wilson's Creek National Battlefield, 6424 West Farm Road 182, Republic, MO 65738-9514; (417) 732-2662; www.nps.gov/wicr

Special considerations: Watch for traffic along park roads.

Finding the trailhead: From Springfield drive west on Walnut Street to the Kansas Expressway. Turn left (south) onto the Kansas Expressway and drive 1.7 miles to Sunshine Street. Turn right (west) onto MO 413/Sunshine and continue 6.9 miles before turning left (south) onto State Highway M. Drive 0.7 mile on State Highway M and then turn right (south) onto State Highway ZZ. After 1.5 miles turn left (east) onto Farm Road 182 and drive just 0.1 mile before turning right (south) into the Wilson's Creek National Battlefield park entrance. Continue onto Tour Road (a gate token can be purchased in the visitor center) and turn left (east) onto the one-way auto tour road. Drive 4.2 miles on the auto tour road to the Bloody Hill parking area and trailhead on the right. GPS: N37 6.346' / W93 24.95'

The Hike

Wilson's Creek National Battlefield commemorates the second major battle of the Civil War and the first battle fought west of the Mississippi River. The site is home to the Wilson's Creek Civil War Museum, which contains a large number of well-interpreted Civil War artifacts and provides in-depth information on the battle that took place here. History buffs will not be alone in their interest of the battle, as the events that unfolded here on August 10, 1861, will certainly pique the attention of nearly all who visit. To learn more about the area, stop by the visitor center and ask about the Cell Phone Audio Tour, which allows visitors with cell phones to learn additional information as they tour the battlefield.

This hike explores the area known as Bloody Hill, where much of the battle took place. As its name suggests, many men, both Union and Confederate, lost their lives here. By the end of the day, more than 2,500 men had been killed or wounded, and despite a high death toll, the Confederate forces were able to claim a victory in the first Civil War battle in Missouri.

Locate the trailhead at stop 7, signed for Bloody Hill, on the Tour Road. From the parking area locate the interpretive signs for the area and begin hiking east on the obvious gravel path. At 0.1 mile pass the Civil War–era cannon, which gives visitors a clue to how troops may have been positioned during the battle; continue east. Shortly after passing the cannon, notice a sinkhole on the south side of the trail that served as a burial site for thirty Union troops.

At 0.25 mile the trail splits; stay right (south). The very short side trail to the left (east) leads to the approximate site where Union General Nathaniel Lyon died during the battle. At 0.3 mile the side trail reconnects to the main trail; continue hiking south.

Come to Wire Road at 0.85 mile; notice the iron bridge over Wilson Creek to the northeast. Confederate troops were camped along the banks of Wilson Creek when Union troops launched a surprise attack in the early-morning hours of August 10. Turn right (south) onto Wire Road. This rocky road once served as the main road between Springfield, Missouri, and Fort Smith, Arkansas.

Pass Edwards Cabin, which marks the site of Confederate General Sterling Price's headquarters at 1.0 mile. Continue hiking southeast, following Wilson's Creek, until you reach the paved Tour Road at 1.35 miles. Turn right (northwest) and walk along the Tour Road, keeping an eye out for auto and bicycle traffic.

At 1.9 miles pass Guibor's Battery. You may wish to detour here to learn more about Captain Henry Guibor's position during the battle. After reading the interpretive information, continue north along the Tour Road until you return to the Bloody Hill parking area at 2.2 miles.

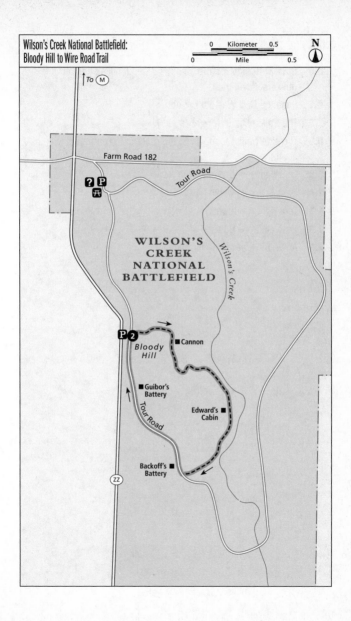

0   Kilometer   0.5

0   Mile   0.5

N

To M

Farm Road 182

Tour Road

WILSON'S
CREEK
NATIONAL
BATTLEFIELD

Wilson's Creek

Cannon

Bloody
Hill

Guibor's
Battery

Edward's
Cabin

Tour Road

Backoff's
Battery

ZZ

Miles and Directions

0.0 Start at the interpretive signs and begin hiking east on the obvious gravel path.

0.1 Pass the Civil War-era cannon.

1.25 The trail splits; stay right (south).

0.3 The side trail reconnects to the main trail; continue hiking south.

0.85 Turn right (south) onto Wire Road.

1.0 Pass Edwards Cabin.

1.35 Turn right (northwest) and walk along the Tour Road.

1.9 Pass Guibor's Battery.

2.2 Arrive back at the parking area.

3 Busiek State Forest and Wildlife Area: Red Trail

This interesting hike features several challenging climbs, the crystal-clear water of Woods Fork Creek, and a cemetery that dates back to the late 1800s.

Distance: 3.1-mile loop
Hiking time: About 2 hours
Difficulty: More challenging due to steep, rocky terrain
Best season: Year-round
Other trail users: Mountain bikers and equestrians
Canine compatibility: Leashed dogs permitted
Fees and permits: No fees; permits required for overnight camping
Maps: USGS Day; trail map may be available at various trailheads
or on Missouri Department of Conservation website.
Trail contacts: Missouri Department of Conservation—Southwest Region, 2630 North Mayfair, Springfield, MO 65803; (417) 895-6880; http://mdc .mo.gov
Special considerations: Area is subject to flash flooding. Hiking access may be limited due to bridge washouts.

Finding the trailhead: From Springfield drive 24.2 miles south on US 65 to Busiek Road. Turn left (east) onto Busiek Road into the Busiek State Forest and Wildlife Area. Continue 0.3 mile on Busiek Road, staying left at the T. Drive another 0.2 mile east to the parking area. GPS: N36 51.731' / W93 13.504'

The Hike

Despite being nestled between Springfield and Branson, Busiek State Forest and Wildlife Area feels far removed from city life. The area offers many recreational opportunities, including camping, hiking, mountain biking, horseback riding, hunting, fishing, and birding. The 2,502-acre forest is just what you would expect in this part of the Ozarks—steep and rocky terrain, rugged trails, and crystal-clear creeks. There are no restrooms, and no water is available. Most of the area is forested, but hikers will notice several glades along the trails. A glade is an open, rocky area with very shallow soil that is dominated by plants. Ozark glades often feature plants and animals that one might expect to see farther to the south and west, such as the prickly pear cactus, tarantula, and roadrunner.

Locate the trailhead and information kiosk on the east side of the large gravel parking area. Notice the information on black bears, which are present, although not often seen, in the area. Black bear sighting have increased in Missouri, particularly in the Ozarks, in recent years. While not a cause for concern, it is important to know how to act in bear country. Following Leave No Trace guidelines on keeping a clean camp and knowing how to act if you do encounter a bear will help keep both hikers and bears healthy and happy. For more information on black bears in Missouri, contact the Missouri Department of Conservation.

Hike northeast through the primitive camping area, passing through a diversely wooded area of black walnut, sycamore, cedar, redbud, pine, honey locust, tulip tree, oak, and elm. At 0.4 mile the trail bends to the north and joins a service road. Continue east on the service road and very shortly come to another camping area. Stay left (north), following the red blazes.

Cross Woods Fork Creek at 0.7 mile. Be prepared to get your feet wet, as flash floods have been known to wash out bridges here. Just after crossing the creek, the trail forks; continue hiking north on the main trail as it begins to climb a moderate hill. At 1.1 miles come to a fork in the trail; turn right (south), following the red blazes as they lead downhill.

At 2.0 miles the trail splits again. Stay to the right (west) and look for the red blazes, which mark the way. After about 0.2 mile reach a somewhat confusing trail intersection where the Red Trail, Yellow Trail, and a shortcut trail meet. Take the trail with the red and yellow blazes, which heads west and downhill. The trail marked with only red blazes heads north and will shorten your hike, leading you back to the camping area and eventually the parking area.

Very shortly after this tricky intersection (2.25 miles), come to another intersection. Again take the trail that leads west and is blazed with both red and yellow.

At 2.6 miles reach Carter Cemetery. The cemetery has gravesites dating back to 1891 and is shared by several local families. Come to a service road at 2.8 miles; turn right and continue hiking north, crossing Woods Fork Creek at 3.0 miles and returning the parking area at 3.1 miles.

Miles and Directions

0.0 Start at the trailhead parking area and hike northeast through the camping area.

0.4 The trail joins a service road; continue east on the service road, passing a few campsites.

0.7 Cross Woods Fork Creek and follow the trail north.

1.1 Come to a fork in the trail; turn right (south), following the red blazes as they lead downhill.

2.0 The trail splits; stay to the right (west) and look for the red blazes.

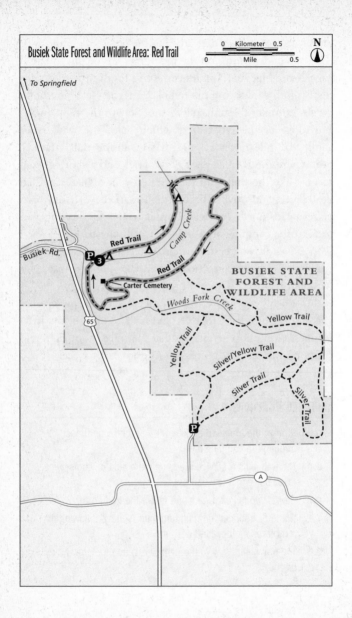

Busiek State Forest and Wildlife Area: Red Trail

0   Kilometer   0.5
0   Mile   0.5

N

To Springfield

Busiek Rd.

Red Trail

Camp Creek

Red Trail

P
3

Carter Cemetery

BUSIEK STATE
FOREST AND
WILDLIFE AREA

Woods Fork Creek

Yellow Trail

Yellow Trail

Silver/Yellow Trail

Silver Trail

Silver Trail

65

P

A

2.2 Reach a trail intersection; take the trail marked with both red and yellow blazes, which heads west and downhill.

2.25 Come to another trail intersection; again take the trail that leads west and is blazed with both red and yellow.

2.6 Reach Carter Cemetery.

2.8 Turn right (north) onto a service road.

3.0 Cross Woods Fork Creek and continue north.

3.1 Arrive back at the trailhead.

4 Busiek State Forest and Wildlife Area: White Trail

Located on the western side of Busiek State Forest and Wildlife Area, the White Trail offers a longer, more challenging trek for hikers wanting to experience the Ozark terrain.

Distance: 4.2-mile lollipop
Hiking time: About 2.5 hours
Difficulty: More challenging due to length and several moderately steep climbs
Best season: Spring through fall
Other trail users: Mountain bikers and equestrians
Canine compatibility: Leashed dogs permitted
Fees and permits: No fees; permits required for overnight camping

Maps: USGS Day; trail map may be available at various trailheads or on the Missouri Department of Conservation website.
Trail contacts: Missouri Department of Conservation—Southwest Region, 2630 North Mayfair, Springfield, MO 65803; (417) 895-6880; http://mdc.mo.gov
Special considerations: Area is subject to flash flooding. Hiking access may be limited due to bridge washouts.

Finding the trailhead: From Springfield drive 24.2 miles south on US 65 to Busiek Road. Turn left (east) onto Busiek Road into the Busiek State Forest and Wildlife Area. Continue 0.3 mile on Busiek Road, staying right at the T. Drive another 0.4 mile west to the parking area. GPS: N36 51.827' / W93 14.176'

The Hike

The 2,502-acre forest is typical of the Ozarks in this part of the state; steep and rocky terrain and rugged trails highlight the area. There are no restrooms, and no water is available. Most of the area is forested, but hikers will notice several glades along the trails. A glade is an open, rocky area with very shallow soil that is dominated by plants and features flora and fauna often associated with the southwestern United States. Hikers in the Ozarks might expect to see prickly pear cacti, tarantulas, or roadrunners. Despite its proximity to Springfield and Branson, Busiek State Forest and Wildlife Area feels quite remote. The area offers many recreational opportunities; camping, hiking, mountain biking, horseback riding, hunting, fishing, and birding are all available here.

The White Trail is located on the west side of the Busiek Sate Forest, near the shooting range. From the parking area cross over Camp Creek and begin hiking northwest on the obvious rock trail.

Keep an eye out for Missouri's most common venomous snake, the copperhead. Since the state is home to nearly fifty species of snakes, hikers visiting the area should become comfortable with the idea of sharing the trails with these reptiles. The Missouri Department of Conservation offers a wonderful free guide on the state's snakes. Learning about these creatures will help you to properly identify snakes and appreciate their unique niche in the ecosystem. Like most snakes, copperheads prefer flight to fight. Unprovoked, they are relatively harmless, so the best practice is just to be aware of where you are stepping, particularly when crossing creeks and rocky hillsides.

The first 0.5 mile of the trail is blazed for both the White and Purple Trails. You will pass through a typical hardwood forest of oak and hickory. You may notice a few honey locust trees also, easily identified by the tree's sharp thorns.

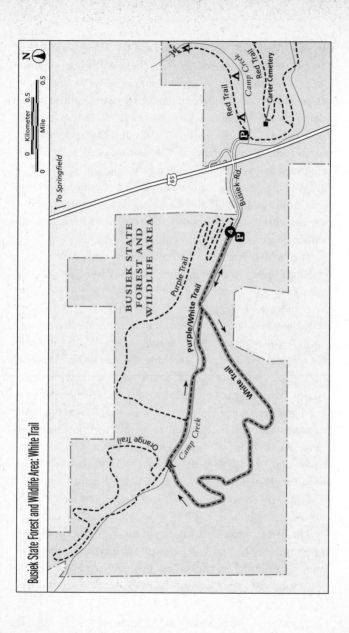

Busiek State Forest and Wildlife Area: White Trail

At 0.55 mile turn left (southwest) to begin the loop section of the lollipop-shaped hike. At 1.35 miles cross a small creek and continue west up a steep ridge, passing through a small grove of eastern cedar trees. Reach the top of the ridge at 1.6 miles. In fall or winter, when there is less foliage, this climb will reward you with a good view. The trail levels out for a bit before descending the ridge at 2.0 miles.

Cross a small drainage near the bottom of the ridge at 2.6 miles, and continue southeast on the trail/service road. At 3.1 miles the White Trail joins the Purple Trail and continues southeast, following the bank of Camp Creek. At 3.8 miles you reach the end of the loop portion of the hike. From here the trail back to the trailhead and parking area should look familiar as you follow Camp Creek back to the trailhead and parking area at 4.2 miles.

Miles and Directions

0.0 Start at the trailhead and follow the obvious rock path northwest.

0.55 Turn left (southwest) to begin the loop portion of the hike.

1.35 Cross a small creek and continue west up a steep ridge.

1.6 Reach the top of the ridge.

2.0 Descend the ridge.

2.6 Cross a small drainage near the bottom of the ridge and continue southeast on the trail/service road.

3.1 White Trail joins the Purple Trail; continue southeast.

3.8 Come to the end of the loop portion of the hike; continue southeast.

4.2 Arrive back at the trailhead.

5 Busiek State Forest and Wildlife Area: Silver Trail (Short Loop)

Located between Springfield and Branson, Busiek State Forest and Wildlife Area makes a fine destination for hiking and other outdoor activities. The Silver Trail features plants and animals common to the rocky Ozark glades in this part of the country. Keep an eye out for prickly pear cacti, tarantulas, lizards, and roadrunners as you cross the small glade.

Distance: 1.8-mile loop
Hiking time: About 1 hour
Difficulty: Moderate due to rocky trail and one long hill climb
Best season: Fall through spring
Other trail users: Mountain bikers and equestrians
Canine compatibility: Leashed dogs permitted
Fees and permits: No fees; permits required for overnight camping
Maps: USGS Day; trail map may be available at various trailheads
or on the Missouri Department of Conservation website.
Trail contacts: Missouri Department of Conservation—Southwest Region, 2630 North Mayfair, Springfield, MO 65803; (417) 895-6880; http://mdc .mo.gov
Special considerations: Area is subject to flash flooding. Hiking access may be limited due to bridge washouts.

Finding the trailhead: From Springfield drive 25.9 miles south on US 65 to State Highway A. Turn left (east) onto State Highway A and drive 0.2 mile to an unnamed gravel conservation area road (the first road on the left). Turn left (north) onto the gravel road and drive 0.2 mile to the parking area. GPS: N36 50.871' / W93 12.935'

The Hike

Named in honor of Dr. Urban and Erma Marie Busiek, the 2,502-acre Busiek State Forest is located between Springfield and Branson. The original 740 acres were purchased from the Busieks' son in 1981, with a portion of the land cost being a donation to the Missouri Department of Conservation. Since then the MDC has purchased the rest of the land making up the area. Campsites, hiking trails, and a shooting range have been developed.

Despite being situated between two of the busiest cities in southwest Missouri, Busiek State Forest and Wildlife Area seems far removed from the often-crowded streets of Springfield and Branson. The area offers many recreational opportunities, including camping, hiking, mountain biking, horseback riding, hunting, fishing, and birding. The forest is typical of what one would expect in this part of the Ozarks—steep and rocky terrain, rugged trails, and clear, gravel-bottom creeks. There are no restrooms, and no water is available.

Most of the area is forested, but hikers will notice several glades along the trails. A glade is an open, rocky area with very shallow soil that is dominated by plants. Ozark glades often feature plants and animals that one might expect to see farther to the south and west, such as prickly pear cacti, tarantulas, and roadrunners. Hikers may also see white-tailed deer, wild turkey, gray squirrel, several species of snakes, and other wildlife more commonly associated with southwestern Missouri. The short loop of the Silver Trail is a particularly good area to explore these glade features.

The trailhead is located southwest of the large gravel parking area. Look for it on the left (north) side of the

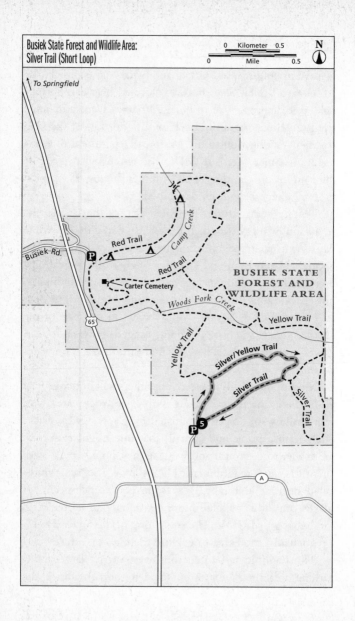

Busiek State Forest and Wildlife Area:
Silver Trail (Short Loop)

0   Kilometer   0.5

0   Mile   0.5

N

To Springfield

Red Trail

Camp Creek

Red Trail

Busiek Rd.

Carter Cemetery

65

Woods Fork Creek

Yellow Trail

BUSIEK STATE
FOREST AND
WILDLIFE AREA

Yellow Trail

Silver/Yellow Trail

Silver Trail

Silver Trail

Silver Trail

5

A

gravel road just before pulling into the parking area. From the trailhead and hiker register, begin hiking north. At 0.1 mile the trail forks; stay left (north) to follow the loop in a counterclockwise direction. The trail is marked with silver blazes painted onto tree trunks. Come to a small glade at 0.4 mile; notice the rocky terrain and prickly pear in this area. The trail forks here; stay right (northeast) and continue on the Silver Trail. You may notice some yellow blazes, as the Silver and Yellow Trails share this section of trail. The trail soon begins a long, rocky descent into a hollow. A hollow is similar to a small valley between two hills or ridges.

At 1.1 miles, near the bottom of the ridge, turn right (southwest) onto the Silver Trail and begin a long ascent out of the hollow. At 1.7 miles come to the end of the loop; turn left (southwest) and return to the trailhead and parking area at 1.8 miles.

Miles and Directions

0.0 Start at the trailhead and begin hiking north on the obvious dirt path.

0.1 Come to a fork in the trail; stay left (north) to follow the loop in a counterclockwise direction.

0.4 Reach a small glade; stay right (northeast) and continue on the Silver/Yellow Trail.

1.1 Reach the bottom of the ridge; turn right (southwest) onto the Silver Trail and begin a long ascent out of the hollow.

1.7 Come to the end of the loop, turn left (southwest).

1.8 Arrive back at the trailhead and parking area.

6 Mark Twain National Forest– Hercules Glades Wilderness Area: Fire Tower Trail to Long Creek

The 12,413–acre Hercules Glades Wilderness Area is located in the Ava District of Mark Twain National Forest. Narrow hollows, open glades, and steep rocky hillsides characterize the area, making it one of the state's finest destinations for those seeking a wilderness experience.

Distance: 4.4 miles out and back
Hiking time: About 2.5 hours
Difficulty: More challenging due to terrain and demanding climbs
Best season: Year-round
Other trail users: Equestrians
Canine compatibility: Leashed dogs permitted
Fees and permits: No fees or permits required
Maps: USGS Ava; printable brochure and map available on the Mark Twain National Forest website

Trail contacts: US Forest Service, Mark Twain National Forest, Ava/Cassville/Willow Springs Ranger District, 1103 South Jefferson St., Ava, MO 65608; (417) 683-4428; www.fs.usda .gov
Special considerations: Outhouse available at trailhead; no drinking water available. Map and compass recommended for all travel in the Hercules Glade Wilderness Area.

Finding the trailhead: From Springfield drive south on US 65 for 5.8 miles to US 60. Turn left (east) onto US 60 and drive 6.6 miles to MO 125. Turn right (south) onto MO 125 and continue for 33.3 miles until you reach MO 125/76. Turn left (east), staying on MO 125/76 for 0.7 mile, and then turn right (south) onto MO 125. Drive 7 miles on MO 125 and turn right (west) into the Hercules Glade Wilderness Area. Drive 0.1 mile to the parking area. GPS: N36 41.069' / W92 53.046'

The Hike

Established as a wilderness area in 1976, Hercules Glades is one of only eight wilderness areas in the state and offers several options for hiking, horseback riding, and camping. There is an abundance of wildlife here, and hikers are likely to see white-tailed deer, squirrels, wild turkeys, rabbits, raccoon, and lizards. Along the limestone outcroppings look for roadrunners, scorpions, and tarantulas. You may also spot the colorful, long-tailed eastern collared lizard soaking up sunrays along the trail. Look for the telltale black or brown marking (collar) around the neck of both the male and the female.

In spring and summer wildflowers such as Indian paintbrush, aster, and spiderwort join the tall prairie grasses in the glades. Like many places in Missouri and the Ozarks, sightings of rattlesnakes and copperheads are possible. Although venomous, bites from these snakes are quite rare. Left unprovoked, these animals are relatively harmless. Keep an eye on children and pets and watch your step, particularly when crossing creeks and walking along rocky hillsides.

There are over 40 miles of trails in the Hercules Glade Wilderness Area. The poorly marked trails here are as rugged as the landscape. While the Lookout Tower Trail to Long Creek is fairly straightforward, any exploration beyond this point will require a map, compass, and topographical map.

You will notice the fire tower as soon as you pull into the parking area. Although it is currently closed to the public,

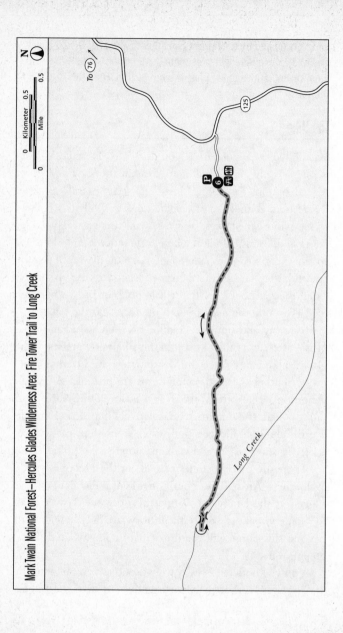

Mark Twain National Forest—Hercules Glades Wilderness Area: Fire Tower Trail to Long Creek

To 76

125

Long Creek

N

0   Kilometer   0.5

0   Mile   0.5

when open the structure offers fine views of the surrounding landscape.

Find the trailhead register on the far west end of the picnic area. Register here and follow the obvious dirt path west along the ridge. You will be hiking through a forested area of mostly oak, hickory, and black walnut trees. In spring it would be hard to miss the bright pink blossoms of the redbud trees found along the trail. At 1.0 mile the trail begins a long decent of the ridge, passing through a small glade at 1.3 miles. From here the landscape alternates between groves of mostly eastern red cedar and grassy groves until you reach the bottomland forest of Long Creek.

At 2.0 miles cross a wet-weather drainage and continue west until you come to Long Creek at 2.2 miles. During certain times of the year, you will be able to enjoy the crystal-clear waters of Long Creek. You may notice a small wooden sign on the west side of the creek marked Fire Tower and pointing in the direction you just came from. This is your clue to turn around and return to the trailhead via the same route.

Miles and Directions

0.0 Start at the trailhead and begin hiking west on the Fire Tower Trail.

1.0 The trail begins a long descent of the ridge; continue west.

1.3 Pass through a small glade; continue west.

2.0 Cross a rocky wet-weather drainage; continue west.

2.2 Reach Long Creek; turn around and return to the trailhead via the same route.

4.4 Arrive back at the trailhead and parking area.

7 Lakeside Forest Wilderness Area: Trails 1 and 2

Located just minutes from the Branson strip, the Lakeside Forest Wilderness Area offers a surprising diversion from the glitter and neon that often characterize this tourist destination.

Distance: 2.9 miles round-trip
Hiking time: About 2 hours
Difficulty: More challenging due to steep terrain
Best season: Year-round
Other trail users: None
Canine compatibility: Leashed dogs permitted
Fees and permits: No fees or permits required
Schedule: Park open daily 7 a.m. to 7 p.m. in summer and 7 a.m. to 5 p.m. through the winter; closed Thanksgiving, Christmas, and New Year's Day
Maps: USGS Branson
Trail contacts: Branson Parks and Recreation Department, 1500 Branson Hills Parkway, Branson, MO 65716; (417) 335-2368; www.bransonparksand recreation.com

Finding the trailhead: From Springfield drive south for 40 miles on US 65 to the MO 76/Main Street exit. Turn right (west) onto MO 76/Main Street and drive 1.1 miles to Fall Creek Road. Turn left (south) onto Fall Creek Road and then make a quick left into the Lakeside Forest Wilderness Area parking lot. GPS: N36 38.367' / W93 14.837'

The Hike

Located within the Branson city limits, the 130–acre Lakeside Forest Wilderness Area sits above the well-known waters of Lake Taneycomo. The area is managed by the Branson Parks and Recreation Department and has been set aside to preserve and protect a portion of the natural beauty found here in the Ozarks. Two separate trails here allow visitors to explore this unique park. Both boast beautiful natural scenery, and each makes a fine day hike. We have linked the two trails together to form a longer day hike through lush woodlands, along steep bluffs, and across rocky glades. A picnic area, restrooms, and water are located near the large gravel parking area.

The trailhead and picnic area are southwest of the parking area. Follow the obvious gravel path south as it winds through the picnic area. At 0.1 mile come to a fork in the trail and continue south on the path signed OWENS TRAIL. This gravel-and-dirt path winds its way through a mostly hardwood forest of maple, oak, and hickory trees. You will notice a few eastern red cedar trees, which are common in many Ozark forests.

At 0.2 mile turn right onto the trail known simply as Trail 2. This natural surface winds southwest through the forest. Look for white-tailed deer and gray squirrels, which feast on the acorns and hickory nuts found in the area. At 0.5 mile come to a rest bench after climbing a modest hill and enter a grove of cedar trees. Inhale and take in the refreshing scent of the forest. Reach a small picnic area at 0.7 mile—a great spot to stop and have a snack. There are two picnic tables and a trash can here.

Hike northeast until you come to a clearing at 1.4 miles; turn right (east) and complete the loop for Trail 2. You will see the parking area to the northeast, but don't stop here. Trail 1 is about to begin, and you will not want to miss the long staircase, grotto, cliffs, and caves that are featured on this hike.

Continue east on the path and reach the trailhead for Trail 1 at 1.5 miles. This out-and-back trail heads south from the trailhead. At 1.6 miles come to another intersection with Trail 2; stay on Trail 1 and continue hiking south. Come to the top of a long stone staircase at 1.75 miles. Turn left to walk down the 315 rugged stairs that lead to the grotto, bluffs, and small caves.

Reach the grotto at 2.0 miles. During rainstorms this massive area becomes a quite impressive waterfall. A sign here reminds you that you will eventually need to climb back up the long stone staircase. Depending on constraints and physical conditioning, some may choose to turn back here. Most will continue along the bluff-side trail to the cave at 2.2 miles before turning around and returning to the trailhead via the same route. At 2.8 miles return to the trailhead for Trail 1; continue north through the picnic area to the gravel parking lot.

Miles and Directions

0.0 Start at the gravel parking lot and follow the gravel path south as it winds through the picnic area.

0.1 Come to a fork in the trail; continue south on the path signed OWENS TRAIL.

0.2 Turn right onto the trail known simply as Trail 2.

0.5 Come to a wooden bench.

0.7 Reach a small picnic area; continue northeast.

1.4 Come to a clearing; turn right (east) and complete the loop for Trail 2.

1.5 Come to the trailhead for Trail 1; turn south to complete the out-and-back portion of the hike.

1.6 Reach an intersection with Trail 2; continue south on Trail 1.

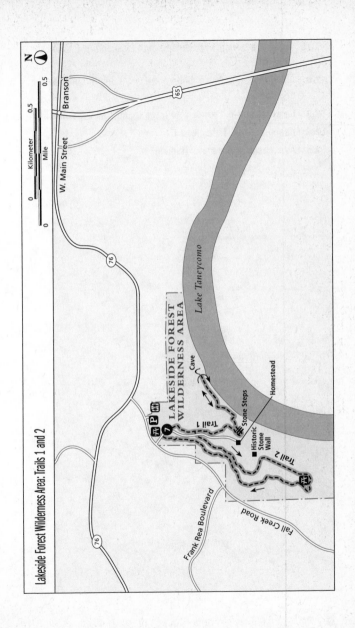

Lakeside Forest Wilderness Area: Trails 1 and 2

1.75 Reach the staircase; continue south, descending the 315 stone stairs.

2.0 Arrive at the grotto; continue northeast along the bluff-side trail.

2.2 Reach the cave; retrace your route to the Trail 1 trailhead.

2.8 Reach the Trail 1 trailhead.

2.9 Arrive back at the gravel parking lot.

8 Ruth and Paul Henning Conservation Area: Homesteaders Trail

Located on the west side of Branson, the Ruth and Paul Henning Conservation Area offers visitors an opportunity to witness the natural and cultural significance of the area.

Distance: 3.6-mile loop
Hiking time: About 2 hours
Difficulty: Moderate due to rocky terrain
Best season: Year-round
Other trail users: None
Canine compatibility: Leashed dogs permitted
Fees and permits: No fees or permits required
Maps: USGS Garber; self-guided trail booklet available at the Springfield Conservation Nature Center, Shepherd of the Hills Fish Hatchery, and Branson Forestry Office
Trail contacts: Missouri Department of Conservation, Branson Forestry Office, 226 Claremont Dr., Branson, MO 65616; (417) 334-3324; http://mdc.mo.gov
Special considerations: Ticks and poison ivy are common in warmer months.

Finding the trailhead: From Springfield drive south on US 65 for 35 miles to MO 465. Turn right onto MO 465 and drive 2.5 miles before turning left (south) onto Sycamore Church Road. Drive 3.8 miles on Sycamore Church Road to the parking area on the left. GPS: N36 41.017' / W93 17.292'

The Hike

The 1,534-acre Ruth and Paul Henning Conservation Area, located in the White River Hills on the west side of Branson, is known for its steep hills, dolomite glades, and oak-hickory forests. Small, desertlike areas known as glades break up the mostly forested landscape. These delicate, sunny glades are home to plants and animals not commonly associated with the Midwest. Eastern collared lizards, scorpions, tarantulas, and roadrunners have all found homes in these Ozarks glades. When glades occur on ridges or knobs, they are often called balds. These areas play an important role in local folk history. They served as rendezvous points for the vigilante group known as the Bald Knobbers after the Civil War.

The area is named for Ruth and Paul Henning, who donated much of the land for the conservation area. Paul Henning, a Missouri native, was the creator of several popular television shows, including *The Beverly Hillbillies, Petticoat Junction,* and *Green Acres.*

This hike focuses on the north side of the conservation area and, as the name suggests, leads visitors past several old homesteads. Be sure to visit the southern side of the conservation area—several short trails there explore the glades.

The trailhead is located on the west side of Roark Creek. From the parking area cross the low-water bridge and locate the trailhead just south of the road. Turn left (southeast) and follow the orange-blazed trail as it meanders along the bank of Roark Creek. At 0.3 mile, just after crossing Dewey Creek, come to a short spur trail the leads to the James Cox homestead. The homestead dates back to the mid-1800s, and visitors can still see what remains of an old fence and a hand-dug well. Return to the main trail and continue hiking south.

Come to the Jones homestead at 1.25 miles. This homestead also dates back to the 1800s. Continue south, passing

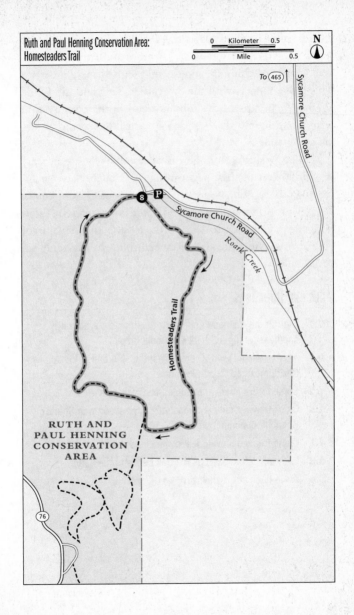

Ruth and Paul Henning Conservation Area:
Homesteaders Trail

0   Kilometer   0.5

0   Mile   0.5

N

To 465

Sycamore Church Road

P
8

Sycamore Church Road

Roark Creek

Homesteaders Trail

RUTH AND
PAUL HENNING
CONSERVATION
AREA

76

several more homesteads as the trail begins to turn to the west. Cross Dewey Creek at 1.8 miles and continue west, very shortly reaching the intersection with Shane's Shortcut. This trail connects with the Streamside Trail and the Glade Trail, which explore the southern end of the conservation area. Continue northwest, passing a small but scenic waterfall at 2.1 miles.

Hikers in spring through early fall will likely see an array of wildflowers as they pass through the open glade at 2.3 miles. Look for white-and-yellow blooms of Queen Anne's lace, Missouri coneflower, and rattlesnake master. From here the trail bends to the north, passing the remains of several more homesteads before returning to the trailhead at 3.6 miles.

Miles and Directions

0.0 Start at the trailhead and follow the orange-blazed trail southeast along the banks of Roark Creek.

0.3 After crossing Dewey Creek, reach the spur trail to the James Cox homestead; continue south.

1.25 Come to the Jones homestead; continue south.

1.8 Cross Dewey Creek and reach the intersection with Shane's Shortcut; continue northwest.

2.1 Come to a small waterfall; continue northwest.

2.3 Pass through a glade as the trail bends to the north.

3.6 Arrive back at the trailhead.

9 Shepherd of the Hills Fish Hatchery: White River Bluffs Trail

Located just 6 miles southwest of Branson, Shepherd of the Hills Fish Hatchery is the largest trout–rearing facility in Missouri. The hatchery produces nearly 400,000 pounds of trout each year, with almost 80 percent of those trout being released into Lake Taneycomo. Both rainbow and brown trout are raised here.

Distance: 1.3-mile loop
Hiking time: About 1 hour
Difficulty: Easy
Best season: Year-round
Other trail users: None
Canine compatibility: Leashed dogs permitted
Fees and permits: No fees or permits required.
Schedule: Hatchery open daily 9 a.m. to 5 p.m.; closed Thanksgiving, Christmas, and New Year's Day. Hours are extended Memorial Day through Labor Day. Guided tours are offered on weekdays from Memorial Day through Labor Day; contact the visitor center for tour hours.
Maps: USGS Table Rock Dam; area map available at Conservation Center
Trail contacts: Shepherd of the Hills Fish Hatchery, 483 Hatchery Rd., Branson, MO 65616; (417) 334-4865; www.mdc.mo.gov

Finding the trailhead: From Springfield drive south for 40 miles on US 65 to the MO 76/Main Street exit. Turn right (west) onto MO 76/Main Street and drive 2.9 miles to MO 165. Turn left (south) onto MO 165 and continue 3.8 miles to Newberry Road. Turn left (south) onto Newberry Road and drive 0.2 mile before turning left (east) at the stop sign onto Hatchery Road. Drive 0.1 mile on

Hatchery Road and then turn right (southeast) onto Belladonna Trail. Continue 0.2 mile to the trailhead parking on the right. GPS: N36 35.912' / W93 17.889'

The Hike

The Shepherd of the Hills Fish Hatchery is owned and operated by the Missouri Department of Conservation (MDC). Located just east of Table Rock Dam, it is bordered on the south by Lake Taneycomo. The hatchery offers tours and is an interesting place to learn about trout culture and other aquatic life. The Conservation Center is open daily and provides information on the flora and fauna of the area as well as the MDC's role in managing wildlife.

In addition to trout, visitors may see white-tailed deer, wild turkey, gray squirrel, raccoon, fox, mink, muskrat, and beaver. In winter visitors will certainly see a large population of vultures, since hundreds of both turkey and black vultures flock to the area each winter to roost.

The hatchery offers several trails, most of which provide fishing access to Lake Taneycomo. The White River Bluffs Trail is the longest trail in the park, and while it does not provide fishing access, it does offer a fine day hike for those interested in further exploring the area.

From the parking area cross Belladonna Trail and locate the trailhead on the north side of the road. Begin hiking on the obvious gravel trail north as it heads into the woods. After a very short walk come to the information kiosk that shows a large trail map and other area information. Continue north until the trail splits at 0.1 mile. Turn left (northwest) to follow the loop in a clockwise direction. The trail traverses a woodland area of mixed hardwoods, eastern

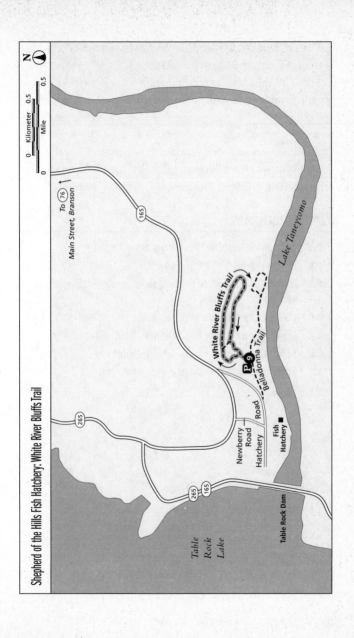

Shepherd of the Hills Fish Hatchery; White River Bluffs Trail

red cedar, and a few shortleaf pine trees. The shortleaf pine is the only pine tree native to Missouri.

At 0.25 mile a side trail splits off to the right (southeast), which shortens the trail; continue hiking east to complete the full trail. Come to another spur trail at 0.5 mile that leads to a private campground; continue east on the main trail. At 1.1 miles come to a connector trail; stay left (southwest). Reach the end of the loop at 1.2 miles; turn left (south) and return to the trailhead and parking area at 1.3 miles.

Miles and Directions

0.0 Start hiking north on the obvious gravel trail.

0.1 The trail splits; turn left (northwest).

0.25 A side trail splits off to the right (southeast); continue hiking east on the main trail.

0.5 Come to another spur trail; continue east on the main trail.

1.1 Come to a connector trail; stay left (southwest).

1.2 Reach the end of the loop; turn left (south).

1.3 Arrive back at the trailhead and parking area.

10 Table Rock State Park: Lakeshore Trail

Connecting the Dewey Short Visitor Center and Table Rock State Park Marina, the Table Rock Lakeshore Trail is an excellent trail for a leisurely stroll along the shores of Table Rock Lake.

Distance: 4.4 miles out and back
Hiking time: About 2 hours
Difficulty: Easy
Best season: Fall through spring
Other trail users: Bicyclists and runners
Canine compatibility: Leashed dogs permitted
Fees and permits: No fees or permits required
Maps: USGS Table Rock Dam; trail brochure available at the Dewey Short Visitor Center and the Table Rock State Park office

Trail contacts: Table Rock State Park, 5272 Highway 165, Branson, MO 65616; (417) 334-4704; http://mostateparks.com/park/table-rock-state-park
Dewey Short Visitor Center, US Army Corps of Engineers, MO 165, Branson, MO 65616; (417) 334-4101; www.swl.usace.army.mil/parks/tablerock/recreation.htm
Special considerations: Watch for bicyclists on the trail.

Finding the trailhead: From Springfield drive south for 42.3 miles on US 65 to the MO 165 exit. Turn right (west) onto MO 165 and drive 7.1 miles to the Table Rock State Park visitor center entrance and parking on the left. GPS: N36 35.596' / W93 18.884'

The Hike

The paved Table Rock Lakeshore Trail, a National Recreation Trail, runs from the Dewey Short Visitor Center to the Table Rock State Park Marina. The relatively flat, wheelchair-accessible trail is open to hikers and bikers and makes for a lovely stroll along the shore of Table Rock Lake. Water fountains, bike racks, benches, and restrooms make this a perfect destination for families with young children or folks just looking for a more relaxed outdoor experience.

Nature lovers will not be disappointed, as the trail is a great place to view plants and wildlife, particularly in the early morning or at dusk. Bald eagles and ospreys are commonly seen in winter, and if you listen closely you might be lucky enough to hear the haunting call of a loon. White-tailed deer, armadillos, fence lizards, and five-lined skinks also can be seen in the area. During spring and summer, hikers will enjoy the bright blooms of butterfly weed, Queen Anne's lace, and tickseed coreopsis, all of which can be found growing along the trail.

The trailhead is at the southwest corner of the Dewey Short Visitor Center. Begin hiking southwest on the obvious, well-signed paved path. Almost immediately the trail enters a mixed-hardwood woodland; look for flowering dogwood, oak, hickory, walnut, and maple. At 0.6 mile come to the *Showboat Branson Belle,* a commercial company offering lake tours, entertainment, and meals. Follow the bright yellow stripes across the parking lot to continue southeast on the trail.

At 1.4 miles reach the Table Rock State Park picnic area. Restrooms, camping, showers, and a boat launch are available here. After the boat launch area, the trail bends to

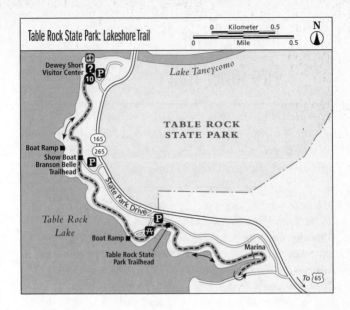

Table Rock State Park: Lakeshore Trail

0 Kilometer 0.5
0 Mile 0.5

N

Dewey Short
Visitor Center

Lake Taneycomo

TABLE ROCK
STATE PARK

Boat Ramp
Show Boat
Branson Belle
Trailhead

165
265

State Park Drive

Table Rock
Lake

Boat Ramp

Table Rock State
Park Trailhead

Marina

To 65

the northeast. Reach the Table Rock State Park Marina at 2.2 miles. This is the end of the trail. Return to the Dewey Short Visitor Center via the same route.

Miles and Directions

0.0 Start at the trailhead and hike southwest on the paved trail.

0.6 Come to the *Showboat Branson Belle;* follow the bright yellow stripes across the parking area, and continue southeast.

1.4 Reach the Table Rock State Park picnic area; the trail bends to the northeast just after the boat launch.

2.2 Reach the Table Rock State Park Marina; return to the Dewey Short Visitor Center via the same route.

4.4 Arrive back at the visitor center.

11 Roaring River State Park: Fire Tower Trail

This loop hike traverses the Roaring River Hills Wild Area and the Roaring River Cove Hardwood Natural Area, both of which provide habitat for several species of plants and animals that are found only in this region of the state.

Distance: 4.3-mile loop
Hiking time: About 3 hours
Difficulty: Moderate due to modest climbs
Best season: Year-round
Other trail users: None
Canine compatibility: Leashed dogs permitted
Fees and permits: No fees or permits required
Maps: USGS Eagle Rock; park map available at park office, nature center, and online
Trail contacts: Roaring River State Park, 12716 Farm Road 2239, Cassville, MO 65625; (417) 847-3742; http://mostateparks.com/park/roaring-river-state-park
Special considerations: Ticks and chiggers are common in warmer months.

Finding the trailhead: From Springfield drive southwest on MO 143 for 17.3 miles. Stay right (southwest) on US 60 and drive another 11.1 miles before turning left (south) onto MO 39. Follow MO 39 for 13.7 miles and then turn right (southwest) onto MO 248. Follow MO 248 for 14.1 miles into the town of Cassville and turn left (south) onto MO 112. Drive 6 miles on MO 112 to the park entrance and continue on MO 112 for 0.9 mile before turning left (east) onto State Highway F. Follow State Highway F for 0.3 mile to Campground #3 and turn right (south) into the area and then make an immediate left into the nature center parking lot. GPS: N36 34.766' / W93 49.828'

The Hike

One of Missouri's oldest state parks, Roaring River State Park offers a wide variety of recreational activities. Perhaps best known for the trophy trout that swim the waters of Roaring River Spring, the park also offers excellent opportunities for hiking, camping, swimming, and just enjoying the natural beauty of the area.

The park is characterized by the type of terrain one would expect to find in the White River section of the Ozarks. Narrow valleys, deep blue springs, mountainlike topography, and interesting rock formations make this 4,000-acre park the perfect day hiking destination. White-tailed deer, striped skunk, mink, and gray fox are common here. The park is also home to several species that are rare or endangered in Missouri, including the Oklahoma salamander, eastern collared lizard, black bear, and long-tailed weasel.

The Fire Tower Trail traverses the Roaring River Hills Wild Area, which provides ideal habitat for many of the park's rare and endangered plants and animals. It also gives hikers an opportunity to view the southwestern border of the Roaring River Cove Hardwood Natural Area, which contains one of the few old-growth oak-hickory forests in the state.

Locate the trail on the south side of the nature center and begin hiking east and then north on the rocky trail. Look for the brown blazes that mark the trail as you walk beside MO 112 for about 100 feet. Come to a gravel parking area on the north side of the road, which is signed for the Fire Tower Trail. Follow the obvious rocky path north as it begins a 0.5-mile ascent of a moderately steep ridge through a hardwood forest.

Roaring River State Park: Fire Tower Trail

Devil's
Kitchen
Trail

Deer
Leap
Trail

Shelter
Cave

Fish
Hatchery

ROARING RIVER
STATE PARK

Lookout Tower

*Roaring
River
Spring*

Fire Tower Trail

Cave &
Spring

11

Nature
Center

Roaring River

At 0.9 mile reach an intersection with a spur that connects to the Deer Leap Trail. Stay right (northeast) and continue along the ridgeline on the Fire Tower Trail. Look for the rare Ozark chinquapin tree as you walk along the ridge. You will reach the old lookout tower at 1.7 miles. Constructed by the Civilian Conservation Corps in the 1930s, the tower provides a good vantage point to take in the tree canopy of the Roaring River Hills Wild Area and Roaring River Cove Harwood Natural Area. Continue hiking southeast along the ridge.

At 2.2 miles the trail begins to descend the rocky ridge. Come to a glade at 2.8 miles; take a moment to note the contrast between this area and the forest you just hiked through as the trail begins to head southwest.

At 3.2 miles the trail turns to the south toward MO 112 and leads to large gravel parking area. Cross MO 112 and find the path heading west on the south side of the road. The trail descends a small hill, crosses a gravel road, and eventually reaches the bank of the Roaring River at 3.4 miles. Continue hiking west until you come to a gate and small parking area at 3.8 miles. Follow the paved park road northwest, past Camp Smokey. Continue northwest on the road until you return to the nature center at 4.3 miles.

Miles and Directions

0.0 Start at the nature center and begin hiking east, then north. Cross MO 112 and come to the gravel parking area on the north side of the road; follow the trail north.

0.5 Reach the top of the ridge.

0.9 Intersection with spur trail that connects to the Deer Leap Trail; stay right (northeast).

1.7 Reach the lookout tower; continue southeast.

2.2 Begin to descend the ridge.

2.8 Come to a glade.

3.2 Cross MO 112; turn right (west) onto the trail.

3.4 Reach the Roaring River; continue west.

3.8 Come to a gate and parking area; continue northwest on the park road.

4.3 Arrive back at the nature center.

12 Roaring River State Park: Devil's Kitchen Trail

Named for a strange rock outcropping that once formed a roomlike enclosure, the Devil's Kitchen Trail is a fun day hike and a good opportunity to explore the interesting geology that is common to this part of Missouri.

Distance: 1.5-mile loop
Hiking time: About 1.5 hours
Difficulty: Moderate due to modest climbs
Best season: Year-round
Other trail users: None
Canine compatibility: Leashed dogs permitted
Fees and permits: No fees or permits required
Maps: USGS Eagle Rock; park map and self-guiding brochure available at the park office and nature center
Trail contacts: Roaring River State Park, 12716 Farm Road 2239, Cassville, MO 65625; (417) 847-3742; http://mostateparks.com/park/roaring-river-state-park
Special considerations: Ticks and chiggers are common in warmer months.

Finding the trailhead: From Springfield drive southwest on MO 143. After 17.3 miles stay right (southwest) on US 60; drive another 11.1 miles before turning left (south) onto MO 39. Follow MO 39 for 13.7 miles, and then turn right (southwest) onto MO 248. Follow MO 248 for 14.1 miles into the town of Cassville, and turn left (south) onto MO 112. Drive 6 miles on MO 112 to the park entrance; continue on MO 112 for another 0.7 mile before turning left (north) onto FR 1135. Follow FR 1135 for 0.4 mile to the parking area and trailhead. GPS: N36 35.448' / W93 50.092'

The Hike

Established in 1928, Roaring River State Park offers a wide variety of recreational activities. While best known for the trophy trout that swim the waters of Roaring River, the park also offers excellent opportunities for hiking, camping, swimming, and just enjoying the natural beauty of the area. Kids and adults alike will enjoy a visit to the fish hatchery and swimming pool.

The park is characterized by the type of terrain one would expect to find in the White River section of the Ozarks. Narrow valleys, deep blue springs, mountainlike topography, and interesting rock formations make the nearly 4,000-acre park the perfect day hiking destination. White-tailed deer, wild turkey, and gray fox are common here. The park is also home to several species that are rare or endangered in Missouri, including the Oklahoma salamander, grotto salamander, eastern collared lizard, and black bear.

Devil's Kitchen Trail allows hikers a chance to view interesting geologic formations up close and personal. The trail begins in an oak-maple forest just west of the parking area. Hike northwest on the obvious rock trail. At 0.1 mile the trail splits; stay right (north) to follow the loop in a counterclockwise direction. Come to an area called The Bench at 0.16 mile. The Bench is an area where two different types of limestone rock meet. As you can see, the lower rock, dolomite, is eroding much slower than the upper rock, forming a benchlike formation.

At 0.2 mile come to Shelter Cave—an example of the kind of cave that was used by bluff-dwellers nearly 10,000 years ago. Continue hiking north, reaching the top of the ridge at 0.6 mile.

Roaring River State Park: Devil's Kitchen Trail

ROARING RIVER STATE PARK

As the trail begins to descend the ridge, notice the grove of shortleaf pine trees—the only native species of pine found in Missouri. Come to Trailside Spring Cave at 0.9 mile. This cave has a small spring emerging from it and provides habitat for several types of creatures, including salamanders.

Just past the cave come to the headliner for this hike: Devil's Kitchen (0.93 mile). Take some time to explore the massive rocks before continuing east on the trail.

As you leave the Devil's Kitchen area, you may notice several shortcuts that bisect the longer switchbacks. Short-cutting switchbacks encourages erosion and trail washouts and kills habitat for plants and animals. Please stick to the main trail.

At 1.15 miles the trail forks; stay left (northeast) to return to the trailhead. Complete the loop portion of the hike at

1.35 miles; turn right and follow the trail back to the trailhead and parking area at 1.5 miles.

Miles and Directions

0.0 Start hiking northwest on the obvious rock trail.

0.1 The trail splits; stay right (north).

0.16 Come to the area known and The Bench.

0.2 Reach Shelter Cave.

0.6 Come to the top of the ridge.

0.9 Come to Trailside Spring Cave.

0.93 Reach the area known as Devil's Kitchen.

1.15 Come to a spur trail; stay left (northeast).

1.35 Complete the loop portion of the hike; turn right.

1.5 Arrive back at the trailhead.

13 Big Sugar Creek State Park: Ozark Chinquapin Trail

The Ozark Chinquapin Trail offers hikers a chance to experience the Elk River Breaks Natural Area. This remote trail offers solitude and the chance to see one of the best remaining upland savannas in the state.

Distance: 3.5-mile loop

Hiking time: About 2 hours

Difficulty: Moderate due to distance and terrain

Best season: Fall through spring

Other trail users: None

Canine compatibility: Leashed dogs permitted

Fees and permits: No fees or permits required

Maps: USGS Noel

Trail contacts: Big Sugar Creek State Park, Big Sugar Creek Road, Pineville, MO; send mail c/o Roaring River State Park, Route 4, Box 4100, Cassville, MO 65625; (417) 847-2539; http://mostateparks.com/park/big-sugar-creek-state-park

Special considerations: No drinking water is available. Ticks and poison ivy are common in warmer weather.

Finding the trailhead: From Springfield drive west on I-44 for 60.2 miles to exit 11A; merge onto US 71 south. Continue on US 71 south for 32.5 miles before exiting right at the Pineville exit. Turn left (east) onto Old US 71 and drive 1.6 miles into the town of Pineville and to Eighth Street. Turn left (east) onto Eighth Street and continue 6.2 miles (Eighth Street becomes Big Sugar Creek Road) to the trailhead parking on the left. GPS: N36 37.29' / W94 17.653'

The Hike

Established in 1992, the 2,000-acre Big Sugar Creek State Park is the only state park that represents the Elk River Section of the Ozarks Natural Landscape Division. Grassy upland prairies, thickly forested ridges, and savannas once dominated southwest Missouri. Now many of those areas have vanished—in particular, the areas known as savannas. Savannas are prairielike grasslands with few trees that require periodic fires to maintain their unique characteristics. Big Sugar Creek State Park is probably the best remaining example of an upland savanna in the entire state. To further preserve the park's natural features, 1,613 acres of the park were designated as Elk River Breaks Natural Area by the Missouri Natural Areas Committee in 2000. Because this is a relatively new park, facilities are limited. When this guide went to press, there was a small information kiosk and outhouse at the trailhead. Plans are under way to further develop the park by adding a day-use area, interpretive structure, camping area, additional hiking trails, and a canoe launch.

The Ozark Chinquapin Trail winds through Elk River Breaks Natural Area. Hikers here can experience the landscape that makes this woodland so special. Shortleaf pine, oaks, and hickory trees grow along the grassy hillsides. Wildflowers, including royal catchfly and purple coneflower, can be found growing throughout the area. Solitude will be easy to find most of the year. In fact, the trail may feel a bit overgrown to the few hikers brave enough to visit in the hottest summer months.

From the parking area the trail heads north along a mowed grass pathway and soon enters the woodland. Look

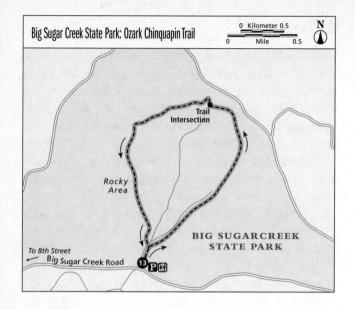

for the trail's namesake tree, the rare Ozark chinquapin, which is found only in the Ozarks. At 0.2 mile the trail forks; stay right (northeast) to follow the trail in a counterclockwise direction. Cross a shallow bedrock stream at 0.3 mile and continue hiking northeast as the trail begins to climb into the upland woodland and glade. At 1.7 miles come to the white Connector Trail, which leads back to the parking area. You can use this connector to shorten your hike. Continue northwest on the Ozark Chinquapin Trail to complete the full loop.

At 2.7 miles cross the rocky bedrock stream again and continue hiking southeast. Come to the end of the loop portion of the hike at 3.3 miles; turn right (south) and continue 0.2 mile to the trailhead and parking area.

Miles and Directions

0.0 Start at the gravel parking area and hike north on the grass pathway.

0.2 The trail forks; stay right (northeast).

0.3 Cross a shallow bedrock stream.

1.7 Come to the Connector Trail; stay right (northwest) to continue on the Ozark Chinquapin Trail.

2.7 Cross the stream; continue hiking southeast.

3.3 Come to the end of the loop portion of the hike; turn right (south).

3.5 Arrive back at the trailhead and parking area.

14 Bicentennial Conservation Area: Multi-Use Trail

This loop hike traverses a thickly wooded area where white-tailed deer, wild turkey, and other woodland creatures can be spotted.

Distance: 5.5-mile loop
Hiking time: About 3.5 hours
Difficulty: More challenging due to length
Best season: Year-round
Other trail users: Mountain bikers and equestrians
Canine compatibility: Leashed dogs permitted
Fees and permits: No fees or permits required
Maps: USGS Neosho East; area map and brochure on the Missouri Department of Conservation website
Trail contacts: Bicentennial Conservation Area, Missouri Department of Conservation, 1510 South Highway 71, Neosho, MO 65850; (417) 451-4158 or (417) 781-2811; http://mdc.mo.gov
Special considerations: No drinking water is available. Ticks and poison ivy are common in warmer months. Watch for mountain bikers and equestrians on the trail. Hunting is permitted in the conservation area; wear blaze-orange or other brightly colored clothing during deer hunting seasons.

Finding the trailhead: From Springfield drive west on I-44 for 54 miles to exit 18A; turn south onto MO 59/US 71. Continue on MO 59/US 71 for 17.5 miles before turning left (south) onto Cemetery Road. Drive 0.5 mile on Cemetery Road and then turn right (west) onto Landis Road. After 0.2 mile turn left (south) onto Doniphan Drive; continue 0.4 mile to the parking area on the left. GPS: N36 50.221' / W94 21.517'

The Hike

Located within the city limits of Neosho, the 721-acre Bicentennial Conservation Area is popular with hikers, mountain bikers, equestrians, and nature lovers. The area has two trails: the short, paved Mort Walker Trail and the longer, natural-surface trail known simply as the Multi-Use Trail.

This area was once part of the Camp Crowder Army Base. Until the 1950s, thousands came here for basic training, including famed cartoonist and University of Missouri graduate Mort Walker. Most famous for creating the *Beetle Bailey* and *Hi & Lois* comic strip series, Walker no doubt used this experience when developing the antics of his *Beetle Bailey* characters.

Despite its lackluster name, the Multi-Use Trail is an excellent choice for a longer, more challenging day hike. Mountain bikers have fallen in love with the rugged path, and each spring the aptly named Le Tour de Tick mountain bike race is held on this trail.

The unmarked trail begins in the woods on the south end of the large gravel parking area, just behind the outhouse. Begin hiking in a generally westward direction, following the path through a thickly forested area. Look for several species of oak trees, including white, black, post, blackjack, and red oaks. Also keep an eye out for poison ivy; the triple-leafed plant is common here and can grow as a vine or a shrub. Anyone hiking anywhere in Missouri should learn to recognize this plant, which is common throughout the state.

Come to a fork in the trail at 0.3 mile; stay to the right and continue hiking southeast. At 0.4 mile the trail bisects a small grove of eastern red cedars and enters an open swath of land, crossing under some power lines.

At 1.0 mile the trail forks again. Stay to the right (northeast) and continue on the main trail, crossing under the power lines at 1.2 miles.

Cross a dirt road (Roark Road) at 1.6 miles and continue east. At 2.0 miles the trail parallels a dirt road and climbs a small hill before turning south back into the woodland.

The trail joins an old gravel road at 2.4 miles. The trail shares this path for 0.1 mile and then continues east.

At 3.5 miles the trail leaves a grassy area and heads northwest into the woods, coming to a barbed-wire fence after a short distance. Follow this fenceline up a short, steep hill and come to a gravel road. Turn right (north) and locate the trail at 3.6 miles as it enters the woods and continues northwest. Cross under the power lines again at 4.1 miles and continue hiking west.

At 4.7 miles cross a small stream just before reaching another old gravel road; follow the trail west into the woods.

Come to another access point for the trail at 5.4 miles near Doniphan Road. Turn left (south) and follow the trail 0.1 mile to the main parking area.

Miles and Directions

- **0.0** Start hiking south and then immediately east on the unmarked dirt-and-rock trail.
- **0.3** Stay right at a fork in the trail, and continue hiking southeast.
- **0.4** Cross through a grove of eastern red cedars and under power lines.
- **1.0** Come to a fork in the trail; stay to the right (northeast) and continue on the main trail.

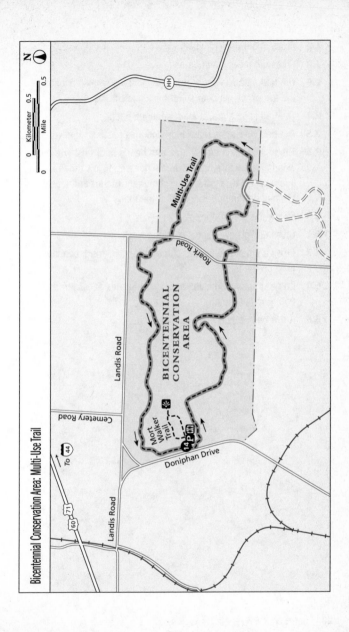

Bicentennial Conservation Area: Multi-Use Trail

1.2 Cross under power lines.

1.6 Cross dirt road; continue east.

2.0 The trail parallels a dirt road and climbs a small hill; near the top of the hill bear south back into the woods.

2.4 The trail joins a gravel road; continue east.

2.5 The trail leaves the road and continues east into the woods.

3.5 The trail leaves a grassy area and heads northwest into the woods. Come to a barbed-wire fence and follow the fence-line up a hill to a gravel road; turn right (north) and locate the trail on the opposite side of the road.

3.6 Follow the trail northwest.

4.1 Cross under power lines; continue west.

4.7 Cross a small stream and come to a gravel road; continue west on the trail.

5.4 Come to a small parking area that provides access to the trail; turn left (south).

5.5 Arrive back at the main parking area.

15 Bicentennial Conservation Area: Mort Walker Trail

Winding through a mixed hardwood forest, the paved Mort Walker Trail offers hikers, birders, and nature photographers an opportunity to enjoy the landscape of southwestern Missouri.

Distance: 0.8-mile loop
Hiking time: About 1 hour
Difficulty: Easy; flat, paved surface
Best season: Year-round
Other trail users: None
Canine compatibility: Leashed dogs permitted
Fees and permits: No fees or permits required
Maps: USGS Neosho East; area map and brochure available on the Missouri Department of Conservation website
Trail contacts: Bicentennial Conservation Area, Missouri Department of Conservation, 1510 South Highway 71, Neosho, MO 65850; (417) 451-4158 or (417) 781-2811; http://mdc.mo.gov
Special considerations: No drinking water is available. Ticks and poison ivy are common in warmer months. Watch for mountain bikers and equestrians on the trail. Hunting is permitted in the conservation area; wear blaze-orange or other brightly colored clothing during deer hunting seasons.

Finding the trailhead: From Springfield drive west on I-44 for 54 miles to exit 18A; turn south onto MO 59/US 71. Continue on MO 59/US 71 for 17.5 miles before turning left (south) onto Cemetery Road. Drive 0.5 mile on Cemetery Road and then turn right (west) onto Landis Road. After 0.2 mile turn left (south) onto Doniphan Drive; continue 0.4 mile to the parking area on the left. GPS: N36 50.246' / W94 21.513'

The Hike

The 721-acre Bicentennial Conservation Area is located within the city limits of Neosho, Missouri. Popular with hikers, mountain bikers, equestrians, and nature lovers, the area offers two options for hiking: The short, paved Mort Walker Trail is a great option for families, people in wheelchairs, or those just wanting an easy, relaxing stroll in a beautiful setting. The longer, natural-surface trail known simply as the Multi-Use Trail offers a more challenging option and is open to equestrians and mountain bikers as well as hikers.

This area was once part of the Camp Crowder Army Base, and the trail is named for famed cartoonist and University of Missouri graduate Mort Walker. Most famous for creating the *Beetle Bailey* and *Hi & Lois* comic strips, Walker completed his basic training here and no doubt used that experience when developing the antics of his *Beetle Bailey* characters.

Locate the trailhead just south of the large pavilion. Follow the obvious paved path northeast through a woodland consisting of oak, elm, sumac, and sycamore. In spring it will be hard to miss the bright pink blooms of the redbud trees that fight for sunlight along the sides of the trail.

At 0.1 mile come to a trail intersection; continue northeast on the paved path. At 0.3 mile come to a wooden bench where a paved spur trail breaks off to the right (northeast). Take this spur 0.1 mile to a wooden boardwalk and overlook platform. There is a bench here, and it is a great area for bird and wildlife viewing. After enjoying this area, return to the main trail at 0.5 mile.

Turn right (west) and notice some large eastern red cedars. Also keep an eye out for poison ivy; the triple-leafed

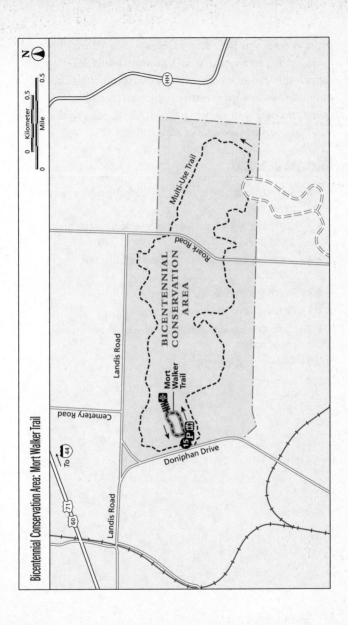

Bicentennial Conservation Area: Mort Walker Trail

plant is common here and can grow as a vine or a shrub. Anyone hiking anywhere in Missouri should learn to recognize this plant, which is common throughout the state. Come to another intersection with a gravel path at 0.6 mile; continue southwest on the paved path. Return to the trailhead and parking area at 0.8 mile.

Miles and Directions

0.0 Start at the parking area and begin hiking northeast on the paved trail.

0.1 Come to a trail intersection; continue northeast on the paved path.

0.3 Come to a bench and a fork in the trail; turn right (northeast).

0.4 Reach a boardwalk and overlook.

0.5 Return to main trail; turn right (southwest).

0.6 Come to a trail intersection; continue southwest on the paved path.

0.8 Arrive back at the trailhead.

16 George Washington Carver National Monument: Carver Nature Trail

This beautiful little trail explores the boyhood home of George Washington Carver. Woodlands, streams, a spring-fed pond, and a tallgrass prairie restoration area are just a few of this trail's highlights.

Distance: 1.1-mile loop
Hiking time: About 1 hour
Difficulty: Easy
Best season: Fall through spring
Other trail users: None
Canine compatibility: Leashed dogs permitted.
Fees and permits: No fees or permits required
Schedule: Park and Carver Discovery Center open daily except Thanksgiving, Christmas, and New Year's Day

Maps: USGS Gramby; trail map available at the visitor center
Trail contacts: George Washington Carver National Monument, 5646 Carver Rd., Diamond, MO 64840; (417) 325-4151; www.nps.gov/gwca
Special considerations: Ticks and poison ivy common in warmer months. Swimming, wading, and fishing are prohibited.

Finding the trailhead: From Springfield drive west on I-44 for 54 miles to exit 18A; turn south onto MO 59/US 71. Continue on MO 59/US 71 for 6.3 miles before turning right (west) onto State Road V. Continue 1.9 miles on State Road V and then turn left (south) onto Carver Road. Drive 0.7 mile on Carver Road to the park entrance and parking area on the right. GPS: N36 59.188' / W94 21.279'

The Hike

Born into slavery near Diamond Grove, Missouri, George Washington Carver went on to gain worldwide recognition as a scientist, botanist, educator, and inventor. His work in agriculture led to peanuts, soybeans, and sweet potatoes becoming major crops in the southern United States.

The George Washington Carver National Monument preserves the site of Carver's boyhood home. The rolling hills, woodlands, prairies, and springs located on the 210-acre site sparked Carver's interest in science and botany. Founded in 1943, this was the first US monument honoring a person other than a president. The on-site Carver Discovery Center interprets the extraordinary life that Carter led.

From the north side of the Carver Discovery Center, begin hiking north on the obvious paved path. The trail bisects a tallgrass prairie restoration area. Look for wildflowers such as prairie rose, purple coneflower, black-eyed Susan, and yarrow. Plants like these sparked Carver's interest in botany at an early age.

At 0.1 mile come to a small log cabin that marks Carver's birthplace. He shared a small cabin, similar to this one, with his brother and mother. When he was just an infant, outlaws kidnapped Carver and his mother, Mary. He was later found in Arkansas, but his mother was never found. After he had been returned to the Carvers, George and his brother, Jim, moved into the Carvers' cabin, which was located nearby.

Continue on the trail, passing the Boy Carver statue and the Carver Spring before crossing the footbridge over Carver Branch at 0.2 mile. Continue northwest to Williams Pond. At 0.3 mile the trail splits. Turn right (northeast) onto the Contemplative Loop Trail, which circumnavigates Williams Pond. The natural beauty and serenity of the area is enough to put most in the mood for contemplation, but for good measure the park service has placed several thought-provoking quotes by Carver along the trail. At 0.5 mile complete the Contemplative Loop Trail; turn right (southwest) and continue on the main trail.

At 0.7 mile come to the 1881 Moses Carver House. Moses Carver built this home after his cabin was destroyed by a tornado. From here continue south through the woodland and then return to the Prairie Restoration Area. Reach the Carver Cemetery at 0.9 mile. Here the trail turns to the left (northeast) and heads back to the Carver Discovery Center at 1.1 miles.

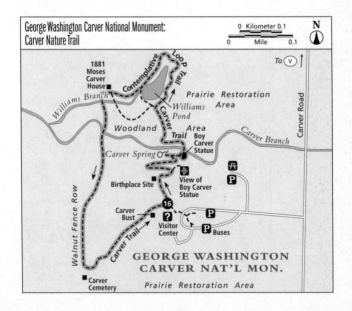

Miles and Directions

0.0 Start at the north side of the discovery center and begin hiking north on the paved footpath.

0.1 Come to a small log cabin that marks the birthplace of George Washington Carver.

0.2 Cross the footbridge over Carver Branch.

0.3 Turn right (northeast) onto the Contemplative Loop Trail that circumnavigates Williams Pond.

0.5 Complete the Contemplative Loop Trail; turn right (southwest) and continue on the main trail.

0.7 Come to the 1881 Moses Carver House.

0.9 Reach the Carver Cemetery.

1.1 Arrive back at the trailhead and the Carver Discovery Center.

17 Little Sac Woods Conservation Area: Oak Hickory Trail

Just a short drive up the road from Springfield, the Little Sac Woods Conservation Area offers a quick retreat on a series of short day hikes. The Oak Hickory Trail meanders through a forest of mixed oaks and hickories and passes a few ponds that are a draw for frog gigging.

Distance: 2.4-mile lollipop

Hiking time: About 1.5 hours

Difficulty: Moderate due to length

Best season: Fall through spring

Other trail users: None

Canine compatibility: Leashed dogs permitted

Fees and permits: No fees or permits required

Schedule: Conservation area closed from 10 p.m. to 4 a.m.

Maps: USGS Walnut Grove; trail maps available at the trailhead

Trail contacts: Missouri Department of Conservation, 2630 North Mayfair, Springfield, MO 65803; (417) 895-6880; http://mdc4.mdc.mo.gov/Applications/MOATLAS/AreaSummaryPage.aspx?txtAreaID=7940

Special considerations: Ticks are common in warmer months. Hunting is permitted in the conservation area; wear blaze-orange or other brightly colored clothing during hunting seasons.

Finding the trailhead: From Springfield drive north on MO 13 for 13.9 to State Highway BB. Turn left (west) onto State Highway BB and drive 2.6 miles to FR 115. Turn left (south) onto FR 115 and continue 1.3 miles to the parking area on the right. GPS: N37 23.285' / W93 23.046'

The Hike

The Little Sac Woods Conservation Area offers 772 acres of forested recreational land. Like many of the conservation areas in Missouri, Little Sac also offers hunting opportunities during designated seasons. Deer hunting is allowed by permit, as is furbearer trapping. The conservation area also offers fishing and frogging in its handful of ponds. In addition to hunting and fishing, Little Sac also offers 7.3 miles of trails to nature lovers and hikers.

From the trailhead parking area, locate the Oak Hickory Trail at the southwest corner of the parking lot and begin hiking south. Follow the white blazes with red writing for the Oak Hickory Trail. After a moderate downhill hike and small creek crossing, you will reach the beginning of the Oak Hickory Trail loop at 0.2 mile. Turn left (south) to begin the loop and to enjoy the thick forest of mixed oaks and hickories. At 0.5 mile the trail crosses a forest service road. Stay right (southwest) to continue on the Oak Hickory Trail. Keep an eye out for deer, wild turkeys, raccoons, and the occasional turtle that is making its way to one of the area's ponds.

Continue hiking through the hardwood forest until the Oak Hickory Trail joins the Boundary Trail for 0.1 mile. At 1.3 miles the two trails part ways, with the Boundary Trail going left (west). Continue on the Oak Hickory Trail to the right (northeast) until you reach the Savannah Trail at 1.5 miles. The Savannah Trail intersects the Oak Hickory Trail from the northwest. Continue straight on the Oak Hickory Trail for another 0.1 mile before the trail makes a sharp right (southeast) turn (1.6 miles). Continue hiking southeast along the grassy trail until the loop portion of the

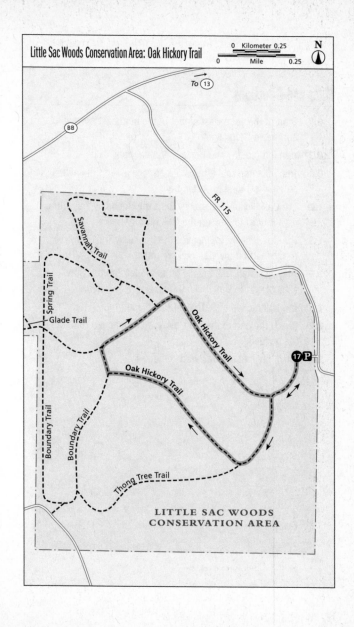

Little Sac Woods Conservation Area: Oak Hickory Trail

0   Kilometer   0.25

0   Mile   0.25

N

To 13

BB

FR 115

Savannah Trail

Spring Trail

Glade Trail

Oak Hickory Trail

Oak Hickory Trail

17 P

Boundary Trail

Boundary Trail

Thong Tree Trail

LITTLE SAC WOODS
CONSERVATION AREA

trail ends at 2.2 miles. Turn left (northeast) to return to the trailhead at 2.4 miles.

Miles and Directions

0.0   Start at the southwest corner of the northeast parking lot and begin hiking south.

0.2   Turn left (south) and begin a gradual uphill hike.

0.5   The trail intersects a service road; continue to the right (southwest) to stay on the trail.

1.2   The Oak Hickory Trail briefly joins the Boundary Trail. Turn right (north) to stay on the Oak Hickory Trail.

1.3   The Oak Hickory Trail leaves the Boundary Trail. Stay right (northeast) on the Oak Hickory Trail.

1.5   The Savannah Trail breaks off to the left (north). Stay straight on the Oak Hickory Trail.

1.6   The trail makes a sharp right (southeast) turn.

2.2   Reach the end of the loop. Stay left (northeast) to return to the trailhead.

2.4   Arrive back at the trailhead.

18 Bennett Spring State Park: Savanna Ridge Trail

Hikers looking to escape the throngs that come to the park to fish will enjoy this getaway. After traveling past the Bennett Spring and accessing the trail, you'll have the hardwood forest almost all to yourself in this beautiful Ozark setting. The trail meanders gently through the forest for an enjoyable day hike.

Distance: 2.6-mile lollipop
Hiking time: About 1.5 hours
Difficulty: Moderate due to length
Best season: Fall through spring
Other trail users: None
Canine compatibility: Leashed dogs permitted
Fees and permits: No fees or permits required
Schedule: Park is open 24 hours. Trails are open sunrise to sunset.
Maps: USGS Bennett Spring; trail guides available in the nature center; maps are also available at the trailhead.
Trail contacts: Bennett Spring State Park, 26250 Highway 64A, Lebanon, MO 65536; (417) 532-4338, www.bennett springstatepark.com
Special considerations: Ticks are common in warmer months; trail may be inaccessible after heavy rains.

Finding the trailhead: From Springfield drive 48.2 miles east on I-44 to exit 129. Turn left (northwest) onto MO 64 and drive 12.1 miles to MO 64A and the park entrance. Turn left (west) onto MO 64A and drive 0.9 mile to Bennett Spring State Park (BSSP) 7. Turn left onto BSSP 7 and drive 0.1 mile before bearing left onto BSSP 2 and continuing another 0.2 mile. Bear right onto BSSP 3 and drive 0.1 mile to the parking area. GPS: N37 42.937' / W92 51.248'

The Hike

Bennett Spring State Park is home to the fourth-largest spring in the state of Missouri. James Brice built the first gristmill here in 1846, but his son-in-law Peter Bennett enjoyed the most success with it. It was the Bennett family for whom the spring, and eventually the state park, was named.

In 1900 the Missouri Fish Commissioner introduced 40,000 mountain trout into the spring to satisfy the growing number of recreationists and fishermen coming to the area. In 1923 a private fish hatchery was built, and in 1924 the state purchased the spring and part of the land to create one of Missouri's first state parks.

Although it's immensely popular with trout anglers, the 3,200-acre park offers much, much more than just fishing opportunities. Visitors can camp in either basic or improved campsites, go swimming in the pool, pick up supplies at the park store, rent canoes to go floating on the Niangua River, or see what is happening at the nature center. Of course there are hiking opportunities as well.

Hikers can make their way over to Spring Hollow to explore the park's backcountry. The 7.5-mile Natural Tunnel Trail is highlighted by the Bennett Spring Natural Tunnel—a collapsed cave that is 15 feet high, 50 feet wide, and 100 yards long. The Savanna Ridge Trail sets out from the same trailhead and offers similar views of the spring branches, bluff tops, hardwood forests, and classic Ozark streams.

The trailhead for the Savanna Ridge and Natural Tunnel Trails is located at the southern end of the parking area. The trails share the same trailhead and begin in the same hiking direction.

From the trailhead kiosk hike northwest along the dirt path following the green arrows that mark the Savanna Ridge Trail. After 0.1 mile reach an old service road and turn left (south) onto the road. Follow the road for only 0.1 mile before turning left (east) again to continue on the now-grassy Savanna Ridge/Natural Tunnel Trail. At 0.3 mile reach the beginning of the loop portion of the hike. Turn right (south) onto the Savanna Ridge Trail and leave the Natural Tunnel Trail for a short while. The trails will reconnect to return to the trailhead later in the hike.

Continue hiking through the hardwood forest south until you come to a white-blazed connector trail that breaks off to the east. Hikers looking for a shorter trek can take this route for a 1.5-mile round-trip.

Continue hiking south past the connector. At 1.3 miles the trail begins to descend the Savanna Ridge. Don't forget your fern identification card so that you can identify some of the beautiful ferns that line the trail during this section.

At about 1.6 miles reach the east end of the white-blazed connector trail; continue hiking to the right (northeast). In another 0.2 mile (1.8 miles) the Savanna Ridge Trail reconnects with the Natural Tunnel Trail. Hikers looking to extend their trip can turn south here.

Turn left (north) to complete the Savanna Ridge Trail loop. After turning left (north), hike along the bottom until the loop portion of the hike ends at 2.2 miles. Continue hiking straight (west) to return to the trailhead at 2.6 miles.

Miles and Directions

0.0 Start at the Natural Tunnel/Savanna Ridge trailhead and begin following the obvious dirt path northwest into the woodlands.

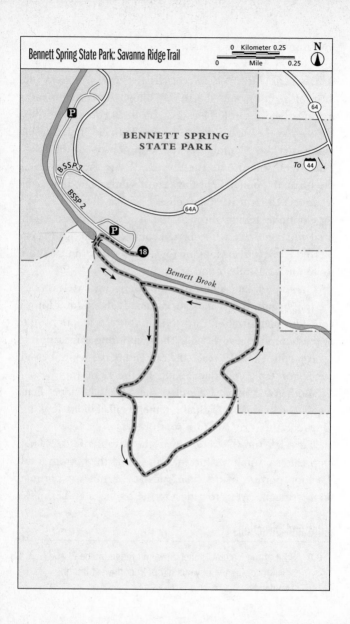

Bennett Spring State Park: Savanna Ridge Trail

0   Kilometer   0.25

0   Mile   0.25

N

BENNETT SPRING
STATE PARK

P

BSSP 1

BSSP 2

P

64A

64

To 44

18

Bennett Brook

0.1 Turn left (south) onto a service road and cross a bridge before heading uphill.

0.2 Leave the service road, turning left (southeast) onto the well-marked Savanna Ridge Trail (green arrows).

0.3 Come to the beginning of the loop; turn right (south) to continue on the Savanna Ridge Trail.

0.8 Intersect the white-blazed connector trail. Stay right (south) on the Savanna Ridge Trail. (**Option:** Bear left (east) onto the connector trail for a 1.5-mile hike.)

1.3 The trail continues down the ridge and passes several ferns and a buckeye tree that may already be turning fall colors as early as July.

1.6 Reach the east end of the white-blazed connector trail; continue right (northeast) on the Savanna Ridge Trail.

1.8 The Savanna Ridge Trail rejoins the Natural Tunnel Trail. Stay left (north).

2.2 Reach the end of the loop. Turn right (west) to return to the trailhead.

2.6 Arrive back at the trailhead.

19 Pomme de Terre State Park: Indian Point Trail

The Indian Point Trail offers a gentle stroll through a beautiful mixed hardwood forest. The trail is highlighted by views of Pomme de Terre Lake from rocky and rugged Indian Point. Hikers wishing to make a day of the hike can stop by the picnic area and beach that can be accessed from the trail.

Distance: 3.1-mile loop
Hiking time: About 2 hours
Difficulty: Moderate due to length
Best season: Fall through spring
Other trail users: None
Canine compatibility: Leashed dogs permitted
Fees and permits: No fees or permits required
Schedule: Park open sunrise to sunset year-round

Maps: USGS Sentinel; trail maps available at the park office
Trail contacts: Pomme de Terre State Park, HC 77, Pittsburg, MO 65724; (417) 852-4291; www.mostateparks.com/park/pomme-de-terre-state-park
Special considerations: Ticks are common in warmer months.

Finding the trailhead: From Springfield drive north on MO 13 for 26.2 miles. Turn right (north) onto MO 83 and drive 2.8 miles to Broadway Street. Turn right (east) onto Broadway Street and drive 0.9 mile before turning left (north) onto State Highway D. Continue 13.7 miles on State Highway D and then stay straight (north) onto MO 64. Drive 7 miles on MO 64 and then turn left (northwest) onto MO 64 Spur. Drive 1.9 miles into the park and to the parking area and trailhead on the left. GPS: N37 52.535' / W93 19.157'

The Hike

Pomme de Terre, literally translated as "apple of the earth," offers myriad recreational opportunities. The 734-acre state park contains an amazing array of terrain, some of the best that Missouri has to offer. The rugged hills of the Springfield Plateau mixed with glades, the Pomme de Terre River, and Pomme de Terre Lake afford recreational possibilities for land lovers and water lovers alike. The 200-year-old post oaks and chinquapin oaks that grow in abundance here are classic indicators not only of the rocky terrain but also that this area was once open woodland at the edge of the Great Plains.

Settlement of the area began in the 1830s, and the Pomme de Terre River was actually the divider between white settlers and the natives. The US Army Corps of Engineers dammed the spring-fed river in the early 1960s to create today's 7,800-acre Pomme de Terre Lake.

Visitors to Pomme de Terre State Park have a couple of options for a pleasant hike. On the Hermitage side of the park, hikers can enjoy a more heavily wooded area that follows rocky bluffs along the lake's shoreline. On the Pittsburg side of the park, where Indian Point Trail is located, hikers get to experience a trek through a savanna woodland. Both sides offer the opportunity to see wild turkeys, deer, purple finches, and prairie warblers.

The Indian Point Trail kiosk is located at the northern end of the trailhead parking area. Begin hiking north on the paved trail as it heads toward an outdoor amphitheater; the pavement quickly ends and turns to a dirt surface. Continue hiking through the open woodland that is abundant with post and chinquapin oaks. At 0.4 mile cross the park road and continue hiking north into the woodland area. After 0.6 mile come to a picnic area on the left (west); turn sharply right (east) to continue on the Indian Point Trail. The trail continues for another 0.2 mile before reaching a restroom on the left (north), a park road (left goes to a beach area), and then a connector trail. After crossing the park road, headed east, pass the red-blazed connector trail that offers a shorter hike. Continue hiking straight (northeast) to stay on the Indian Point Trail.

At 1.4 miles reach the spur trail that leads out to Indian Point. Take a few moments to walk out onto the rugged and rocky peninsula and take in the views before returning to the trail; continue south. After hiking through the woodland area and taking in several views of the lake, reach a bench at 2.7 miles that offers a nice place to rest while watching the folks down in the marina prep their boats.

Return to the trail and hike southwest for 0.3 mile before reaching the southern end of the red-blazed connector trail (3.0 miles). Continue hiking west past the connector trail and then across the park road. Return to the trailhead at 3.1 miles.

Miles and Directions

0.0 Start at the trailhead kiosk and travel north on the Indian Point Trail, signed with blue arrows.

0.4 Cross the park road and continue north on the trail.

0.6 Reach a picnic area to the west. The trail turns sharply right (east).

0.8 Come to the Pittsburg Beach Area. Continue hiking east across the park road and quickly approach the red-blazed connector trail that heads south. Continue hiking straight (east).

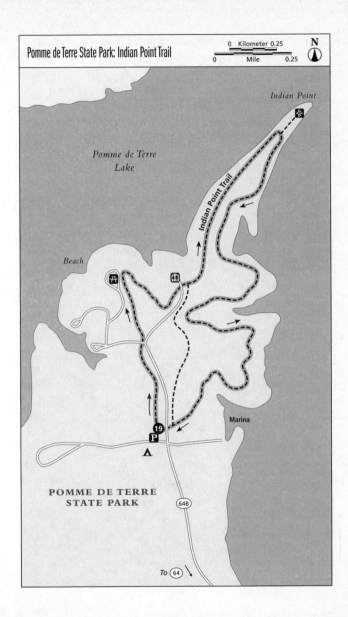

Pomme de Terre State Park: Indian Point Trail

0 Kilometer 0.25
0 Mile 0.25

N

Indian Point

Pomme de Terre Lake

Indian Point Trail

Beach

Marina

19 P

POMME DE TERRE
STATE PARK

64B

To 64

1.4 Reach a spur trail that leads to Indian Point. After checking out the scenery, return to the trail and continue hiking south on the Indian Point Trail.

2.7 After hiking near the shore for a short stretch, come to a bench with a good view of the marina.

3.0 The red-blazed connector trail intersects from the north. Continue west on the Indian Point Trail and then cross the park road.

3.1 Arrive back at the trailhead.

20 Ha Ha Tonka State Park: Devil's Kitchen Trail

A short hike through a state park well known for its numerous hiking trails, the Devil's Kitchen Trail packs many of the park's tourist sites into one hike. A large sinkhole, glades, chert woodlands, a natural bridge, and views of old castle ruins are just some of the wonders this trek has to offer.

Distance: 1.4-mile loop

Hiking time: About 1.5 hours

Difficulty: Moderate due to rocky trails and climb

Best season: Fall through spring

Other trail users: None

Canine compatibility: Leashed dogs permitted

Fees and permits: No fees or permits required

Schedule: Park open 7 a.m. to sunset Apr through Oct and 8 a.m. to sunset Nov through Mar

Maps: USGS Ha Ha Tonka; trail and natural area guides available in the visitor center

Trail contacts: Ha Ha Tonka State Park, 1491 State Highway D, Camdenton, MO 65020; (573) 346-2986; http://mostateparks.com/park/ha-ha-tonka-state-park

Special considerations: Ticks are common in warmer months.

Finding the trailhead: From Springfield drive 48.2 miles east on I-44 to exit 129. Turn left (northwest) onto MO 64 and drive 1.7 miles to MO 5. Turn right (north) onto MO 5 and drive 19 miles to Dry Hollow Road. Turn left (west) onto Dry Hollow Road and continue another 3.7 miles to State Highway D. Turn left onto State Highway D and then make an immediate left into the trailhead parking area. GPS: N37 58.423' / W92 45.749'

The Hike

The area that is now Ha Ha Tonka State Park was almost Missouri's first state park. Governor Herbert Hadley proposed the idea in 1909, but it was rejected. Ha Ha Tonka didn't become a state park until 1978—surprising when you consider that this area is known as "Missouri's karst showcase."

Features like a 70-foot-wide, 60-foot-long natural bridge, 150-foot-deep sinkholes, numerous caves, and even old castle ruins would seem to make this area a shoe-in for a state park. In 1903 Robert Snyder was so impressed with the area that he purchased more than 5,000 acres here to build a European-style castle as a retreat. Snyder began building his elaborate getaway in 1905 but was killed in one of the country's first automobile accidents only a year later. His sons finished the work, and the castle functioned as a hotel until 1942, when it was accidentally burned to the ground.

Hikers on the Devil's Kitchen Trail get a few glimpses of the old castle ruins and have the option to visit the ruins via connecting trails. The 1.4-mile loop also passes some of the most amazing natural features the park has to offer. The park that was carved from stone will have you wanting more after you hike the Devil's Kitchen Trail.

From the trailhead parking area, begin hiking south on the gravel trail. The trail slowly rises up a moderate slope and quickly intersects Acorn Trail at 0.1 mile. Stay to the right and continue hiking south, following the brown blazes for the Devil's Kitchen Trail. The trail continues through an open woodland savanna and begins going downhill, reaching the Devil's Kitchen and Promenade at 0.4 mile.

Continue hiking through the Kitchen and make your way up and across a large opening in the rocks. Step across the gap, make your way along the ledge that circles the sinkhole, and eventually begin climbing out of the Kitchen. At 0.7 mile cross Post Office Road; continue hiking northwest until you reach the Post Office Shelter Area at 0.9 mile. Turn right (north) to follow the footprints across State Road D into the Spring Trail parking area, and proceed down the stairs where the Devil's Kitchen Trail and Spring Trail join each other briefly. At the bottom of the stairs turn right (east); continue to 1.1 miles, where the Spring Trail splits away to the left (northwest) and the Devil's Kitchen Trail continues northeast.

At 1.2 miles turn right (northeast) to continue following the brown blazes. Shortly thereafter take a sharp right (southeast) at a picnic area to cross over the natural bridge. The Colosseum sinkhole will be to your left and right as you cross over the bridge. At 1.4 miles cross State Road D again and return to the trailhead parking area.

Miles and Directions

0.0 Start at the trailhead kiosk and begin hiking south on the gravel trail up a moderate slope.

0.1 Acorn Trail splits to the lift; stay right (south) on the Devil's Kitchen Trail following the brown blazes.

0.4 After descending a hill into the Devil's Kitchen and Promenade, continue past a cave and take a big step across an opening in the rocks before walking along a ledge above the sinkhole.

0.7 Cross Post Office Road to continue on the Devil's Kitchen Trail.

0.9 Turn right (north) at the Post Office Shelter Area and follow the footprints across State Highway D. Continue down a set of stairs on the Devil's Kitchen/Spring Trail.

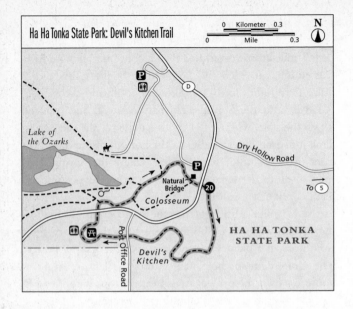

Ha Ha Tonka State Park: Devil's Kitchen Trail

Lake of
the Ozarks

Dry Hollow Road

To 5

Natural
Bridge

Colosseum

HA HA TONKA
STATE PARK

Post Office Road

Devil's
Kitchen

1.0 At the bottom of the stairs, bear right (east) to stay on the Devil's Kitchen Trail.

1.1 The Spring Trail splits to the left (northwest); continue northeast on the Devil's Kitchen Trail.

1.2 Turn right (northeast) and continue following the brown blazes. Soon take another sharp right (southeast) to cross over the natural bridge.

1.4 Cross State Highway D and arrive back at the trailhead parking area.

Hike Index

About the Authors

JD Tanner grew up playing and exploring in the hills of southern Illinois. He has earned a degree in Outdoor Recreation from Southeast Missouri State University and an advanced degree in Outdoor Recreation from Southern Illinois University in Carbondale. He has traveled extensively throughout the United States and is the coordinator for outdoor recreation at San Juan College.

Emily Ressler-Tanner grew up in southeastern Missouri and southeastern Idaho. She spent her early years fishing, hiking, and camping with her family. In college she enjoyed trying out many new outdoor activities, graduating from Southern Illinois University with an advanced degree in Recreation Resource Administration.

Together they have climbed, hiked, paddled, and camped all over the United States. They coinstructed college-level outdoor recreation courses for several years before joining the staff at the Leave No Trace Center for Outdoor Ethics as Traveling Trainers. They have written revisions for two books for FalconGuides: *Best Easy Day Hikes Grand Staircase-Escalante* and *Hiking Grand Staircase-Escalante*. Other Falcon Guides they have authored include *Best Easy Day Hikes St. Louis* and *Best Hikes near St. Louis*. They currently reside in northwestern New Mexico.